Nationalism
in Latin America

Borzoi Books on Latin America

General Editor
LEWIS HANKE
University of Massachusetts, Amherst

Nationalism in Latin America

EDITED WITH AN INTRODUCTION BY

SAMUEL L. BAILY

Rutgers University

Alfred A. Knopf　　New York

THIS IS A BORZOI BOOK
PUBLISHED BY ALFRED A. KNOPF, INC.

First Edition

98765432

Copyright © 1971 by Samuel L. Baily

All rights reserved under International and Pan-American Copyright Conventions. Published in the United States by Alfred A. Knopf, Inc., New York, and simultaneously in Canada by Random House of Canada Limited, Toronto.

Distributed by Random House, Inc., New York.

Library of Congress Catalog Card Number: 77–88156

Manufactured in the United States

To

❦

Arthur P. Whitaker, who as
Director of the Rockefeller
Foundation–sponsored Argentine
Nationalism Project of the
University of Pennsylvania and as
a scholar and teacher has done
so much to encourage the study
of nationalism in Latin America

Acknowledgments

I am indebted to Lewis Hanke for his interest, his encouragement, and his criticisms as the book took form. I also wish to thank the following people who have helped by making suggestions for readings to be included in the work, or who have read parts of the manuscript: Norman Berzon, E. Bradford Burns, David C. Jordan, Albert Michaels, Noreen Stack, William Svec, Frederick Turner, Arthur P. Whitaker, and Winthrop Wright. Mario Bacigalupo, Frank Dauster, and José Vázquez Amaral very kindly assisted me with some of the translations. Finally, I am again indebted to my wife, Joan, who has greatly improved this work with her suggestions.

Contents

C) *1945–present*

Nationalism
in Latin America

Introduction

An increasingly large number of scholars are arguing that nationalism is the most important single force in Latin America today, yet they have not been able to provide us with a precise, universally acceptable definition of the term nor have they been able to tell us very much about nationalism.* We are often told that all groups—whether of the left, center, or right—appeal to nationalism and seek to exploit it for their own ends; that nationalism is as important a determinant of policy and action in Bolivia, Cuba, and Mexico as it is in Argentina and Brazil; and that we cannot understand contemporary Latin America without comprehending the idea of nationalism. We are not told, however, what nationalism is, how to determine when it exists, how to distinguish it from other phenomena, or how to isolate its effects on any given historical situation. The student of nationalism is therefore in the awkward position of writing about a vague idea which he cannot describe precisely nor comprehend fully and which in the end he must admit might not exist in a clearly identifiable form at all.

The problem arises from the fact that most of us have observed and read about a peculiar force which we label nationalism, but although our intuition, bolstered by some empirical evidence, tells us this force exists and is important, we have so far been unable to grasp its full meaning. The vagueness, complexity, and widespread use of what we call nationalism has even led some to argue that perhaps everything is nationalism and therefore the concept is meaningless.

The idea of nationalism is vague and complex, but my own investigations have convinced me that it does exist as an

---

* See the bibliographical note at the end of the book.

identifiable concept, that it is indeed the most important single force operating in Latin America today, and that although we cannot grasp its totality nor define it with precision, we can study and begin to understand it. To recognize the limits of our knowledge and conceptions and the difficulties of analysis does not mean we should give up in despair. On the contrary it suggests the need for new and imaginative approaches to the study of nationalism and for more investigations of the idea as it has been manifested in various times, places, and forms. Only with a large number of monographic studies of examples of nationalism will someone at some future date be able to make the necessary generalizations which will answer many of our questions.

The purpose of this book is to enable the college student to gain some understanding of what a variety of people mean when they speak of nationalism in Latin America and to stimulate him to study the idea further. Basically I am trying to set forth an approach to the study of nationalism which includes a description of its historical development in the Latin American context and of the wide variety of its manifestations and uses. It also includes the posing of the kinds of questions one might ask in the attempt to understand it. This study does not provide a precise, universally acceptable definition of nationalism nor does it set forth a model of the growth and development of nationalism. Instead it confines itself to the description of and questions about nationalism in Latin America—primarily about nationalism in twentieth-century Argentina, Brazil, and Mexico—which hopefully will lead to precise definitions and effective workable models.

The point of departure for this descriptive examination is the early nineteenth century. Between 1810 and 1825 all of Latin America, except Cuba and Puerto Rico, broke the bonds that for more than three hundred years had tied it to Spain and Portugal and declared its political independence. This act destroyed an all-embracing system of political, economic, and social authority symbolized by the king, but it created no equivalent substitute for this authority. During the Colonial Period there were struggles and protests of various kinds and for a variety of reasons, but almost all men recognized the ultimate right of the king to rule. Once the king was removed, the issue arose as to who or what should inherit his far-reaching authority; who or what should be the arbiter of disputes among groups and individuals within society.

Since the early part of the nineteenth century Latin Americans have sought an acceptable substitute for the unquestioned authority of the king. Individuals and groups have struggled with each other in their efforts to establish a new communal identity and legitimate authority. During most of the nineteenth century the struggle took place between factions of the elite white native ruling groups which frequently assumed the labels of "liberals" and "conservatives." Conservatives generally wished to perpetuate the colonial system, but with themselves, rather than Spaniards or Portuguese, as leaders (see Document 5). Liberals, on the other hand, rejected the political role of the Church and other aspects of the colonial structure and sought to substitute for it what they believed to be a progressive system modeled on that of England, France, or the United States (see Document 3). Although both groups believed that the native elite should govern, neither one respected the right of the other to rule in its behalf. As a result both used force to obtain control of society and to settle disputes within it. In most countries, the formal political structure —the numerous constitutions, the political parties, and the elections—had little meaning; whoever could muster the greatest force ruled. With the exceptions of Brazil and Chile, changes of government were frequent and unpredictable because there was no accepted procedure for transferring authority from one person or group to another.

The rapid industrialization of much of Europe during the nineteenth century had an important effect on the Latin American search for legitimate authority. The European countries, particularly England, needed the raw materials and markets that Latin America could supply. Large numbers of Europeans emigrated and large amounts of private European capital were invested to develop an infrastructure in many countries and this helped stimulate the commercialization of agriculture, the development of mining, the process of urbanization, and the emergence of the middle and lower socioeconomic groups.

In the late nineteenth and increasingly in the twentieth centuries these new groups competed with the traditional native elites for the right to exercise political authority. They refused to permit the elites to rule in their behalf, and their challenge added a new dimension to the search for legitimate authority. Now it was a question of finding authority acceptable not only to factions of the elite, but also to the middle and lower socioeconomic groups. This search, begun nearly 160 years ago, has not yet ended. The problem of establishing acceptable authority in the Latin American countries will not very likely be resolved for some time to come.

The most significant force that has emerged to replace the authority of the king has been nationalism. The primary function of nationalism in Latin America has been to create nations. Today the nation is what Rupert Emerson refers to as the "terminal community," that is, "the largest community which, when the chips are down, effectively commands men's loyalty, overriding the claims both of the lesser communities within it and those which cut across it or potentially enfold it within a still greater society." [1] The nation "effectively commands men's loyalty" because it represents a broad consensus of society on fundamental values and procedures. If it exists, the nation provides its members with a sense of communal identity; it becomes the source of unquestioned authority; and it provides legitimacy for the acts of men and governments.

In the large majority of Latin American countries, unlike most European countries, no such broad consensus has yet emerged and the nation, strictly defined, does not exist. Many groups in each of the countries have attempted and continue to attempt to create a national consensual community, but for the most part they have failed and there is little agreement on what values and procedures each nation would stand for or what membership in a national community would mean. There are few common interests or broadly based institutions that might bind together the diverse elements of contemporary Latin American societies.

Competing nationalist groups claim that they speak for an emerging national consensus and that their interests are the authentic interests of the future nation. Very often these groups, in their efforts to establish the nation and to support their claim to be the genuine representative of this nation, seek to gain control of the state. The group that controls the state cannot represent the nation if the nation does not exist, but control of the state very often gives this group distinct advantages over its competitors: money, police and military support, direct access to the communications media, and a chance to win broader support by performing services for the population. As a result, much of the study of nationalism in Latin America must focus on those who control or seek to control the state.

In the abstract, nationalism in Latin America has developed as the force engendered by those seeking to answer the search for legitimate authority by creating the nation. It is absolutely essential to keep in mind, however, that in each country this development has proceeded at a different pace, that it has been used by different groups and individuals for different purposes, and that it has produced widely divergent results. Since nationalism is so varied, it must be studied within its various historical contexts.

The Historical Development of Nationalism

The Colonial Period

Hans Kohn writes, "Nationalism as we understand it is not older than the second half of the eighteenth century," and most authorities agree with him.[2] Moreover, nationalism emerged later in Latin America than it did in Europe. During the Colonial Period of Latin American history we therefore cannot correctly speak of nationalism, but we can discuss a number of ideas, sentiments, and attitudes which later became important in the emergence and formulation of the idea.

Perhaps most importantly, this period established a specific past of colonial rule associated with the Catholic Church, the Spanish and the Portuguese, the system of mercantilism, an elitist social hierarchy and, for the most part, the effective subjugation of the native peoples and of the Negroes brought over as slaves. In other words, the Colonial Period constitutes the past for the National Period in Latin America and the legacy of that past has had a significant impact on the development of nationalism.

The noted Mexican historian, Daniel Cosío Villegas, referring to the Colonial Period, suggests that "three centuries of this rule necessarily left on American man and his land an indelible mark of intervention from outside America. They also left the seeds of ultranationalism." [3] Cosío Villegas' emphasis on outside intervention is important, but one must also keep in mind the other abovementioned negative elements of the colonial system itself. It is impossible to understand such things as the intense anticlericalism and antiracism of many of Latin Americas' nationalists without understanding the nature and functions of the colonial system.

Related to this is a more positive aspect of colonial history. Nationalism in Latin America has its roots in the growing self-consciousness of the native elites who in the seventeenth and eighteenth centuries developed a sense of separate interest or identity from that of the mother countries. It was a feeling of distinctness and self-reliance most often associated with a local community or area, or with a vague cultural concept of America. How far one wishes to go back to identify this feeling is a matter of individual judgment. It can be argued that there were isolated manifestations of such attitudes during the sixteenth and seventeenth centuries, but these feelings do not become at all widespread among the native cultural elites until the second half of the eighteenth century. For the most part this sense of separate identity is closely related to the spread of the ideas of the Enlightenment, and these ideas are most notable from the time of the reigns of Charles III of Spain (1759–1788) and of José I of Portugal (1750–1777).

Barbarosa Lima Sobrinho, in his book *Desde quando somos nacionalistas,* argues that the initial manifestation of Brazilian nationalism came during the period of the Dutch occupation of the Northeast (1630–1654), but that the most important and widespread early manifestation of the phenomenon was that of the anti-Portuguese variety of the eighteenth century which had its roots in the vehement anti-Portuguese poetry of the seventeenth-century poet Gregorio de Matos. This nationalism, Lima Sobrinho claims, was based on the conflict—for the most part economic— of interests between the mother country and the colonists which produced a feeling among the latter of distinct interests and identity. The War of Mascates (1710–1711), in which the Brazilian planters of Olinda struggled with the Portuguese merchants of Recife, is an important early manifestation of this conflict.

The feeling of self-consciousness is well documented for New Spain (Mexico) by Xavier Tavera Alfaro in his book *El nacionalismo en la prensa mexicana del siglo XVIII.* He points out that Mexican newspapers of the late eighteenth century are important to the study of nationalism. They were edited by natives, they sought to serve the interests of New Spain, and they manifested the self-consciousness of the Mexicans. One of the most influential newspapers he discusses is the *Gazeta de Literatura de México* edited by the distinguished Mexican, Joseph Antonio Alzate Ramírez. The significance of the paper is suggested in the Prologue to the first edition of 1788, where Alzate sets forth its aims: to point out the importance of Mexico, its customs and history to the world; to demonstrate the high level of

culture and science in the area; and to serve the *patria* or
fatherland.

Some natives developed a self-consciousness during the
second half of the eighteenth century, but before this feeling
could emerge into a distinct nationalism many things had
to take place.

The Struggle for Independence

The student of nationalism must be careful not to overestimate the strength of the separatist tendencies that developed during the Colonial Period. Before 1810 there were
few manifestations of a desire to establish political independence. Furthermore, the Independence Movement was
sparked by forces outside Latin America. In 1807 and 1808
Napoleon Bonaparte sent his armies into Portugal and
Spain. The Braganzas, the Portuguese royal family, fled to
Brazil. The presence of the Braganzas and the elevation of
Brazil to the status of kingdom in 1815 stimulated the
pride and sense of importance of the Brazilians. João VI
returned to Portugal in 1821 leaving his son, Pedro, to rule
Brazil. It was Pedro, under the influence of such Brazilian
nationalists as José Bonifácio, who led the Brazilian Inde-
pendence Movement.

In Spain the situation was a bit more confusing. Napoleon succeeded for a time in playing Carlos IV and his son
Fernando VII against each other and in placing his brother,
Joseph Bonaparte, on the throne of Spain. The Independence Movements in Spanish America began as demonstra-
tions of loyalty to the deposed Fernando VII and were only
later converted into movements whose goal was complete
separation.

Several results of the struggle for independence are important for this study. First of all, the actual fighting of the
Wars of Independence intensified anti-Spanish and anti-
Portuguese feeling among the native-born. The violently
anti-Spanish speeches of native leaders such as Simón Bolívar
and Bernardo O'Higgins were more than rhetoric; they ex-

pressed an intense hatred of the Spanish overlords which grew as they fought to protect their lives (see Document 1).[4]

Closely related to this anti-Iberian sentiment was a strong feeling of Americanism. Bolívar, José de San Martín, José Bonifácio, and other native leaders developed a sense of continental solidarity in the face of a common enemy which has since been labeled "continental nationalism." The term "continental nationalism" implies some contradiction because Latin America is made up of a number of sovereign states and the "terminal community" for those living in the area cannot be the continent and the nation-state at the same time. Nevertheless, the feelings of Latin American solidarity and conventional nationalism, strong forces throughout most of the history of independent Latin America (see Documents 12 and 16), may indeed have complemented each other.[5]

Two other results of the Independence Movement which were central to the development of nationalism were the creation of theoretically sovereign political states and the destruction of the authority of the king. Those who controlled the states assumed the powers of the king, that is, the power to govern, to tax, to maintain order, and so on, but they were unable to assume his complete authority. The states became the physical basis for the creation of the national community, but the destruction of the unquestioned authority of the king and the failure to establish a new legitimate authority created a situation, as mentioned above, in which nationalism—or conceivably something else—was needed to bind together the fragmented communities and to legitimize authority. Brazil, of course, was an exception. There the transition from colony to sovereign state was smoother because the Portuguese prince became the Brazilian Emperor.

Nineteenth-Century Latin America

The major change brought about by the Independence Movement was the substitution of native elites for Spaniards and Portuguese at the top of the political hierarchy. The economic structure remained much the same with England replacing Spain and Portugal as the "colonial" economic power. The native elites dominated politics and society, and although they fought among themselves they united in the face of any challenge from below. This system of neo-colonialism prevailed with but slight modifications in most of Latin America throughout the nineteenth century and in some areas into the twentieth century.

More specifically, neocolonialism meant looking abroad for solutions to Latin America's problems, and nationalism, a European import, was no exception. The problem, as Charles W. Anderson points out, was that "the modern world conceives of no alternative maximum independent political status other than the nation-state. Yet the adoption of the forms and trappings of statehood by the small elite to which such status makes a difference does not create a nation." [6] Arthur P. Whitaker and David C. Jordan's description of the earliest variety of Latin American nationalism, or old bourgeois nationalism, suggests the extent of the reliance of the elite nationalists on foreign solutions to their problems. The old bourgeois nationalists, they explain, believed that "the best way to strengthen the nation was to draw as fully as possible on foreign investments, foreign enterprise, and foreign culture," and one may add, foreign political institutions and ideas.[7]

Looking at specific countries we can observe that nationalism was probably stronger in Argentina and Mexico than it was in Brazil. Throughout most of the century (1822–1889) Brazil maintained the monarchy. This traditional colonial institution provided the unquestioned authority and the bonds that held together the newly created state. Nevertheless, benign, romantic, and slightly anti-Portuguese nationalism emerged (see Document 2) along with anti-British and at times anti-Spanish American nationalism.

Argentina and Mexico were, from the beginning, divided into antagonistic groups; nationalism provided at least some theoretical unity among those participating in the continu-

ing struggle for control of their fragmented societies. Iron-
ically, as Daniel Cosío Villegas points out, "The individuals
and political groups who favored 'centralism' always bore
a 'reactionary' and unprogressive stamp, that is, they wished
to delay the advance towards real independence by retaining the forms of Spanish government . . ." [8] The centralism
expressed by the outstanding Mexican Conservative Lucas
Alamán (see Document 5) was never associated with nationalism, while the federalism of the Liberal Mexican
president, Benito Juárez, became closely identified with
nationalism. In Argentina the situation was somewhat different because both the xenophobic nativism of dictator Juan
Manuel de Rosas and the liberal centralism of President
Domingo F. Sarmiento manifested important elements of
nationalism. In both countries, however, the liberal groups,
which dominated the political arena in the latter part of
the century, rejected the Hispanic past and instead looked
to England, France, or the United States for models from
which to create Mexican and Argentine nation-states.[9]

None of these nationalists was very successful in creating
the nation-state because of the barriers that stood in their
way. These barriers, which existed in all of the Latin
American countries to a greater or lesser degree, had a
strong negative impact on the development of nationalism
during the first half of the century. Perhaps the most important barrier to the development of nationalism was
localism. Geography—the high mountain ranges, the jun-
gles, and the lack of navigable rivers—encouraged localism
especially when central governments were unwilling or
unable to do anything for the local communities. Loyalty
to the region or the *patria chica* was more important than
loyalty to the state (see Document 6), and therefore many
states were forced to adopt a federal form of organization.

Personalism was a second barrier to the development of
nationalism during much of the nineteenth century and
later too. The formal institutions of government, for the
most part imported from abroad, were weak. Ideology was
relatively unimportant. The *caudillo*, the informal charis-

matic leader who ruled because he was physically able to, dominated politics. Without modern methods of mass communication (railroads, roads, radio, and television), he generally ruled over only a small area. The net result of the caudillos under these circumstances was to re-enforce localism and to prevent the development of a new loyalty to a national community.[10]

A third obstacle to the development of nationalism was the strong class distinctions that existed throughout the nineteenth century. Independence substituted native-born whites for Spaniards and Portuguese, but this did not fundamentally alter the traditional social structure. Nationalism to the extent that it existed was essentially a doctrine of the upper class and was never very widespread in society. The rigid class structure, and the fear of what the spread of nationalism to other classes might do to that structure and to the privileged people at the top, served to limit it.

Fourth, the Church—controlled by the Vatican, staffed to a considerable extent by foreign priests, and strong at the local level—was a barrier to the development of nationalism. Even though the native elites disagreed about what powers the Church would assume in the independent states of Latin America, the Church continued to exercise much influence, particularly at the local level. The Church, in addition to its control over spiritual life, usually controlled education, medical facilities, and charitable institutions. It was also a major source of borrowed money. As a result, at the local level the priest often had greater authority than did the central or state governments. On the other hand, the Church's cosmopolitanism seemed to dictate ultimate loyalty to something beyond the state. Thus, the efforts of the Church very often served to strengthen localism and cosmopolitanism and to undermine nationalism.

And finally, the rejection by many Latin Americans of the past as a basis for unity proved to be at least a temporary barrier to the development of nationalism. As the Mexican philosopher Leopoldo Zea suggests, while Europe was searching for the type of community it would need in the future, Latin America was debating its past. He observes, "Only people who have not assimilated their history can continue to feel threatened by their past." [11] European nationalists found the past a source of strength upon which to build, but for many Latin American nationalists this option did not seem open (see Document 9).

In spite of the abovementioned obstacles, a number of factors worked in favor of the development of nationalism. For the most part these favorable factors were stronger during the second rather than the first half of the nineteenth century. First, numerous wars stimulated feelings of nationalism, for as Gerhard Masur correctly observes, although territorial struggles and wars were not as important for the creation of nationalism in Latin America as they were in Europe, they were, nevertheless, of some significance.[12] The Argentine-Brazilian War (1825–1828), the Peruvian-Chilean-Bolivian confrontation (1839), the Mexican-American War (1846–1848), the French Intervention in Mexico (1862–1867), the Paraguayan War (1865–1870), and the War of the Pacific (1879–1883) demonstrated the need for national unity in the face of foreign threats, thereby stimulating loyalty to these respective states (see Documents 4 and 7).

Second, the development of a sense of distinct identity which we noted during the second half of the eighteenth century and during the Independence Movement grew stronger during the nineteenth century. By the late nineteenth century, men like the Cuban patriot José Martí rejected Sarmiento's view that the best way to develop the nation was to utilize foreign enterprise and culture, and argued instead that Latin Americans must look within if they were to develop their nations (see Document 8). And in Brazil, the literary critic Sílvio Romero looked within to find his country's own culture.

Third, the drive to modernize, as manifested by the Argentine liberals of the second half of the nineteenth century and by the Mexican *científicos* and the Brazilian positivists at the end of the century, created many of the physical prerequisites for the development of an integrated national community. Particularly in Mexico, Brazil, and Argentina, but in other countries as well, the governments and foreign private capitalists built thousands of miles of railroads and roads and constructed new harbors and modernized old ones. These developments increased communications within the country and with Europe, and made it increasingly possible for a central government to rule effectively.

And finally, the process of miscegenation, or racial mixture, helped stimulate the development of nationalism. Four hundred years of miscegenation created a new group of people, neither Indian nor European—the mestizos— who could look only to the emerging nation-state for a sense of communal identity. Although the extent of miscegenation varied from country to country, the mestizos in every country needed to some degree a new type of community with which to identify (see Document 10). In Brazil and in the Caribbean, miscegenation was more complex due to the infusion of African blood, but it also served to stimulate nationalism.[13]

Twentieth Century

The vague feelings of nationalism that developed during the nineteenth century were, for the most part, limited to the native elites. In the twentieth century these feelings became more pronounced, varied, and widespread. The content of the nationalisms was more precisely defined and the idea spread in differing degrees to most levels of society, including the lower socioeconomic groups.

The emergence of the newer forms of nationalism in twentieth-century Latin America was closely related to the process of modernization which had begun during the second half of the previous century. Karl Deutsch's concept of "social mobilization" is helpful in explaining why. Social mobilization, according to Deutsch, is the process of change that occurs in countries developing from traditional to modern ways of life. In the early stages of this process, traditional

social, economic, and psychological ties, such as the consensus of the native elites that bound together the traditional society, are underminded and/or destroyed. Large seg-
ments of the population are uprooted or mobilized. As a
result, these persons seek to develop new community patterns that might provide a sense of personal identity and a
means for protecting their interests.[14] The new forms of
nationalism developed among the mobilized groups as they
attempted to establish a national consensus on the basis
of their ideas and interests.

For purposes of analysis it is helpful to divide the twentieth century into three chronological periods: 1900 to
1930, 1930 to 1945, and 1945 to the present. These periods
are no more than general guidelines, and there is an over-
lapping of issues among them. But a rough chronological
breakdown of the twentieth century does enable the student
to consider the relationship of particular historical events
to the development of nationalism, and to focus more precisely on the predominant trends of nationalism at any
given moment.

1900 to 1930

A number of new issues emerge within this period that
had an important impact on the development of nationalism. First of all, the expansion of the United States'
political influence and economic interests into the Caribbean and Central America provoked a strong anti-North
Americanism. In the last decades of the nineteenth century,
the United States, in the name of national security, asserted
its hegemony in the Caribbean. This involved, among other
things, complicity in Panama's separation from Colombia,
the construction of the Panama Canal, and the occupation
of Cuba, Haiti, the Dominican Republic, and Nicaragua.
At the same time, with the burdens upon England because
of World War I, United States capital began to replace
British capital in many Latin American countries.

Anti-North Americanism focused not only on the political

and economic influence of the United States, but also on its cultural impact. The Uruguayan José Enrique Rodó, in his famous work *Ariel,* attacked the utilitarianism and materialism of the United States and insisted that Latin Americans emphasize things of the spirit.[15] The Argentine Manuel Ugarte warned Latin Americans of the threat of Anglo-Saxon materialism to their Hispanic spiritualism and urged that they unite to oppose it (see Document 12). This anti-North-Americanism was stronger in Argentina and Mexico than it was in Brazil where men like the Baron of Rio-Branco, the Minister of Foreign Relations from 1902 to 1912, dedicated themselves to encouraging a growing Brazilian-American friendship, but there too anti-Americanism had been voiced as early as 1893 by Eduardo Prado in his book *A ilusão americana.*[16]

A second issue that had an important effect on nationalism was that of race and nationality. With the influx of foreign immigrants in some parts and the increased blending of races in others, the question arose as to who constituted the nationality? In Argentina José Ingenieros, defending Sarmiento's position that the racially mixed gaucho represented barbarism while the Europeans represented civilization, argued that the large number of Spanish and Italian immigrants attracted by the policies of the liberals were the basis of the emerging *raza argentina.*[17] Others, concerned about the growing influence of the European immigrants in Argentine society, urged that something be done to protect traditional Argentine values and culture. *Martín Fierro,* (1872), the epic poem by José Hernández about the life of the gauchos of the pampas became increasingly popular during the early decades of the twentieth century. And, between 1906 and 1916, Ricardo Rojas developed a nationalism which rejected the cultural significance of the numerically important European immigrants. Rojas replaced Sarmiento's dichotomy of civilization and barbarism with his theory that the basic struggle in Argentine history was between exoticism and indianism, between foreign and native influence (see Document 15).

Although there was considerable European immigration to the southern part of Brazil, antiforeignism there was never as strong as it was in Argentina. Nevertheless, a form of nativism called *sertanismo*—the defense of the values and life of the people of the *sertão* (the backlands)—did emerge. This idea, which combined nativism and social justice for the masses, was most forcefully expressed by Euclides da Cunha in his book *Os Sertoẽs* (translated under the title *Rebellion in the Backlands*) (see Document 11). He looked to the interior as the "real" Brazil and to the man of the interior as the "real" Brazilian. Indeed, at that very moment João Capistrano do Abreu was revising Brazilian historiography by indicating that the frontier, not the coast, had been the greatest single factor shaping Brazil's development.

In Mexico as in Peru the search for the roots of the nationality went back to the pre-Columbian period. One of Mexico's most influential theorists, José Vasconcelos, argued in his book *La raza cósmica* and in his "Discurso a Cuauhtémoc" that the genuine Mexican race must draw on the strengths of the Indian as well as the Spaniard to produce the cosmic race of the future. Vasconcelos reinforced these ideas when as Minister of Education under Alvaro Obregón (1920–1924) he encouraged Diego Rivera and other Mexican artists who explored native themes to paint their murals on the walls of many public buildings. In Peru, Víctor Raúl Haya de la Torre, one of the founders of the APRA party (Alianza Popular Revolucionaria Americana) placed even greater emphasis on the Indian as the basis of the Peruvian nationality (see Document 16).

The third issue of importance to emerge within this period was economic nationalism. The rise of economic nationalism was related to the rise of representatives of middle-sector groups to political power—Hipólito Yrigoyen in Argentina, Arturo Alessandri in Chile, Plutarco Elias Calles in Mexico, and José Batlle y Ordóñez in Uruguay. During this period economic nationalism was based primarily on the notion that the nation owned the subsoil and

natural resources of a country and that the good of the
nation prevailed over the rights of private property. Article
27 of the Mexican Constitution of 1917 (see Document 13)
clearly sets forth this idea as the "social function" of property. This concept has also been expressed in the Uruguayan
Constitution of 1917, the Brazilian Constitution of 1934, the
Colombian Constitution of 1936, the Cuban Constitution
of 1940, and the Argentine Constitution of 1949.

Economic nationalism also affected specific policies during this period. Such policies could be seen in the creation
in 1922 of Yacimientos Petrolíferos Fiscales (YPF), the Argentine government oil corporation, and by the multiple
decrees and laws of Venustiano Carranza, Alvaro Obregón
and Plutarco Elias Calles to establish control of the Mexican
oil industry. Economic nationalism was used by various
groups in Chile (see Document 14). It also emerged in
Brazil during the 1920s.

1930 to 1945

The important influences on the development of nationalism during this period were the world depression, the rise
of fascism, and World War II. Economic nationalism became a major issue in Brazil during the years following the
depression. It was repeatedly appealed to by Getúlio Vargas
(1930–1945), who argued that to protect the national interest, the government, without rejecting foreign capital, must
gain control of important industries and in particular the
steel industry (see Document 17). In Bolivia, Colonel David
Toro seized all of the Standard Oil Company's holdings on
March 17, 1937. In Mexico, economic nationalism reached
a peak on March 18, 1938, when President Lázaro Cárdenas
expropriated the large foreign-owned oil companies which
he believed had challenged the sovereignty of the Mexican
government. In Argentina, the government made concessions to England in the Roca-Runciman agreement and in
other agreements which further strengthened foreign control
over the Argentine economy. Although groups from the

extreme left and right protested, economic nationalism did not have nearly the impact there that it did in Mexico and Brazil.

The question of race and nationality took on a new dimension during this period. Formerly the issue was one of the fusion of Indians and Europeans. In Brazil, however, there was a large Negro and mulatto population which had developed as a result of several hundreds of years of slavery. In 1933, the Brazilian Gilberto Freyre published his now classic *Masters and Slaves*. In this book he pointed out the importance of the Negro to the development of Brazilian society and culture, and in so doing introduced the concept of social democracy (the miscegenation of Negro and white) as the basis of the Brazilian nationality (see Document 18). In a sense Freyre was doing for Brazil what Vasconcelos and others had attempted to do for Mexico—to postulate a mixed race as the genuine basis of the country's nationality.[18]

Not all aspects of the racial issue were as positive as those advanced by Freyre. In the north of Mexico and in the south of Brazil, colonies of Orientals emerged. The question naturally arose as to whether the social democracy of Brazil and the *raza cósmica* of Mexico included Asians. Mexico has had a tradition of opposition to immigration which might explain limited hostility to the Chinese. But the government of the state of Sonora—where most of the Chinese in Mexico lived—went beyond limited hostility in treating the Orientals as inferior beings who, if they mixed with the Mexicans, would debilitate the race.[19]

The rise of fascism in the world influenced the development of nationalism in Latin America. Many of the political struggles of the period were viewed as struggles between democracy and fascism. Influenced by the ideas of Charles Maurras, José Antonio Primo de Rivera, and to some extent by those of Benito Mussolini in Italy, many Latin American right-wing elements developed a doctrine that associated Christianity, Hispanic values, the corporate state, and rule by an elite with nationalism (see Document 20). In Argentina this right-wing nationalism gained considerable influence during the 1930s and early 1940s, and its supporters helped bring Juan Perón to power. In Brazil, this movement was manifested in the rise of the Integralist Party of Plinio Salgado and in the Estado Nôvo (1937–1945) of Getúlio Vargas. In Peru, the statesman-historian, Víctor Andrés Belunde, set forth another version of the same doctrine in a book entitled *Peruanidad*. And although these ideas had less influence in Mexico than they did in Argentina or Brazil, they were manifested in the thoughts of some of the supporters of the 1940 opposition presidential candidate, General Juan Andreu Almazán.

In some countries the left wing also attempted to use nationalism to further its cause. In a 1936 speech before the Mexican workers, the Marxist labor leader Vincente Lombardo Toledano clearly sought to capture Mexican nationalism for the proletariat (see Document 19). In Argentina, a group called the Fuerza de Orientación Radical de la Joven Argentina formed within the Radical Party in 1935 in order to stimulate the adoption of a left-wing nationalist program. In addition, a popular-front atmosphere prevailed for a time in Argentina as Radicals, Socialists, and Communists joined with the labor movement to set forth a popular antifascist nationalism.[20]

And finally some mention should be made of the influence of the United States in the development of nationalism in Latin America. For the most part the Good Neighbor Policy, the struggle between fascism and democracy, and World War II blunted the strong anti-North Americanism of the previous period, but a few groups and individuals continued the attack. For example, the famous Mexican muralist Diego Rivera continued to criticize North American imperialism in his works.[21] In addition, a small group influenced by Leon Trotsky argued that the real issue was not fascism versus democracy, but one of opposition to imperialism and foreign control of any sort. This group had an impact on some of the Marxist nationalists who emerged in Argentina and other countries after the war.[22]

1945 to the Present

The main issues during this period have been the impact of World War II, economic development, and the Cold War. Most importantly, popular or populistic nationalism, which had emerged in Mexico before, became more widespread and more influential. The urban workers, and to some extent the rural peons, gained political importance and power and claimed that they were the embodiment of the "general will" and the genuine representatives of the nation. In Brazil, Vargas continued to expand the base of nationalism by appeals to the workers. In Argentina, Juan D. Perón found much of his support among the migrants from the rural areas who lived in the cities, and he consciously articulated a popular nationalism and set forth the goal of a workers' nation (see Document 24). The Bolivian Revolution of 1952 involved the *campesino* in the affairs of the national community for the first time (see Document 22). And in Cuba, Fidel Castro used a violently anti-United States popular Marxist nationalism to legitimize his regime (see Document 27).

Economic nationalism has recently become more intense and influential and has, as previously, been to a considerable extent a response to United States economic policy toward the area. Since 1945 most of the Latin American countries have wanted to develop their own industry. To do this they have had to establish tariffs to protect their infant industries, to create a Latin American Common Market area, and to obtain massive financial aid along the lines of the Marshall Plan for Europe. Between 1945 and 1960 the United States did not share the Latin American countries' analysis of the situation. The United States argued that Latin Americans could better develop their economies in the long run by maintaining low tariffs and by gaining investment capital exporting raw materials. In addition, until recently the United States refused the Latin Americans' requests for massive financial aid. The negative response of the United States to the Latin American desire to industrialize has created a new cause for strong feelings of anti-Americanism, and has given new meaning to economic nationalism.

This feeling was well expressed by the United Nations Economic Commission for Latin America under the leadership of the Argentine economist Raúl Prebisch and the Mexican economist Víctor Urquidi. Neither man rejects the use of foreign capital in the development of Latin America, but both believe that Latin America must industrialize and that foreign powers must not interfere with that process (see Document 21). In Brazil this idea was expressed by members of the Instituto Superior de Estudos Brasileiros, a group formed under the aegis of the Ministry of Education in 1955 to stimulate and promote national development. Hêlio Jaguaribe, a former member of this group, makes the case for economic development under the leadership of the national bourgeoisie (see Document 25).[23]

The Cold War has had an impact on nationalism in Latin America which has often been expressed in the effort to establish a neutral foreign policy. Clearly this was part of the meaning of Juan Perón's "Third Position" between capitalism and communism. It was also behind the abstention of Brazil, Bolivia, Chile, Argentina, Mexico, and Ecuador on the vote to exclude Cuba from the Organization of American States in January 1962. One of the most articulate and forceful spokesmen for the idea was Jânio Quadros, President of Brazil from January to August of 1961 (see Document 26).

Finally, some mention should be made of the military and nationalism in Latin America. In countries like most of those in Latin America where no procedural consensus exists, the armed forces often act as the arbiters of disputes among individuals and groups within society. Partially as a result of this role, the armed forces have come to envision themselves as the special protectors of their emerging nation (see Document 23). There is a wide variety of ideological positions within the various armed forces of Latin America, and these positions are reflected in the kind of nationalism they might set forth. The important point is that the military in Latin America has used and will continue to use nationalism to help it achieve its goals.[24]

Guidelines for the Study of Nationalism

To facilitate the study of nationalism, let me pose the following questions as an analytical guideline:

2. *What were the causes of the development of nationalism in each country?* Was nationalism the result of external threats or of conflicting political, social, and economic interests within society? Was it made possible by improved communications within society? Was it the product of the "uprooting" of large numbers of people due to urbanization, immigration, and so on?

3. *What were the functions of nationalism?* By whom was it used and for what purpose or purposes? Was it externally directed or an integrating force to bind together a fragmented society? Was it used as a source of legitimacy for competing political groups? Was it used by individuals to gain their own personal ends? What effect did it have on social, political, and economic policy? What are the relationships among the various functions of nationalism?

Is it possible to place the various nationalisms into functional categories? K. H. Silvert suggests the following such categories: (*a*) nationalism as patriotism—this "refers to love of country and national community . . . [and] to the collection of symbols expressing this love"; (*b*) nationalism as social value—this "refers to the norm defining the loyalty due to fellow citizens and to the secular state as the ultimate arbiter of all conflicts of public interest"; (*c*) nationalism as ideology—this refers to "those explicit bodies of thought employing the symbols of nationality in order to promote actions intended at least partially to glorify the nation as a good in itself." [25] In addition we might consider nationalism as an integrating force, nationalism as a defensive force against outside threats, etc.

4. *What were the relationships of nationalism to the stages of social, political, and economic development of each country?* Was nationalism externally aggressive at a certain stage of economic development and an integrating force at another? Should we make comparisons between countries at similar stages of economic development rather than at specific points in time? Is there more similarity between nineteenth-century Mexico and twentieth-century Peru than between twentieth-century Mexico and Peru? Can nationalism develop in a pre-industrial society? Can there be a nation without a democratic form of government? To what extent does this depend on the definition of democracy?

5. *To what extent was nationalism felt by the inhabitants of each country and to what extent did it influence their behavior?* In the nineteenth century, nationalism was not widely felt and was to a considerable extent a doctrine of different elites. In many Latin American countries of the twentieth century—but certainly not in all—the idea of nationalism spread to the urban masses and to some extent to the rural masses as well. Has this changed the nature of nationalism? How has this affected the behavior of the masses? How have different kinds of nationalism influenced behavior? How has cultural nationalism changed education? How has economic nationalism changed development policy and practice? How has popular nationalism changed political development?

6. *What descriptive categories of nationalism can we reasonably establish for Latin America?* Do Carlton J. H. Hayes's general categories of nationalism (Humanitarian, Jacobin, Traditional, Liberal and Integral) [26] fit the Latin American situation? Arthur P. Whitaker and David C. Jordan feel that the following categories are more appropriate for Latin America: (*a*) Traditional-rural nationalism—a kind of nostalgic nativism designed to rid Latin America of

the cultural hegemony of Europe; (*b*) Old bourgeois nationalism—a mild nationalism concerned with national uni-
fication and marked by political and economic liberalism
and cultural cosmopolitanism; (*c*) New bourgeois nationalism—a form of economic nationalism that allows for a
wide role for private capital and private enterprise but re-
stricts foreign capital and favors a modified statism; (*d*)
Populistic nationalism—the fusion of nationalism with
social revolution; and (*e*) Nasserist nationalism—a military-
socialist nationalism closely akin to the populistic variety
but stressing the dominant role of the armed forces.[27] In
addition the student might consider such categories as economic nationalism, cultural nationalism, and aristocratic
nationalism. Do these categories overlap? How does one define each of these categories? What do such classifications
tell us and what do they not tell us about nationalism?

7. *To what extent are Brazilian nationalisms similar to
or different from the nationalisms of Spanish America?*
Should we, for example, compare economic or popular nationalism in Brazil with economic or popular nationalism
in Mexico and Cuba, or is there something distinct about
all Brazilian nationalisms when contrasted with those of the
Spanish-speaking countries of Latin America? If there are
differences between Brazilian and Spanish American nationalisms, what accounts for these differences?

8. *To what extent are Latin American nationalisms similar to or different from nationalisms in the rest of the
world?* To what degree are Latin American nationalisms
outgrowths of European nationalisms? Which nationalisms
in which European countries have most influenced Latin
America? How? Are Latin American nationalisms more akin
to those of the United States than to those of the African
and Asian countries that have received their political independence more recently? Why?

Unfortunately it is easier to ask questions about nationalism than to answer them and in this sense the readings
are unsatisfactory. They do not answer some of the above

questions at all and others they answer only in part. These readings should be considered as a starting point for an analysis of nationalism in Latin America and the student who wishes to pursue the subject can do so by consulting the bibliography at the end of the book.

Introduction Bibliography

1. Rupert Emerson, *From Empire to Nation* (Boston: Beacon Press, 1962), pp. 95–96.
2. Hans Kohn, *The Idea of Nationalism* (New York: Macmillan, 1960), p. 3.
3. Mildred Adams, ed., *Latin America: Evolution or Explosion?* (New York: Dodd, Mead, 1963), p. 115.
4. Robin A. Humphreys and John Lynch, in their book *The Origins of the Latin American Revolutions, 1808–1826* (New York: Knopf, 1965), provide additional examples of the nationalism of the creoles during this period.
5. For a further discussion of continental nationalism see Arthur P. Whitaker and David C. Jordan, *Nationalism in Contemporary Latin America* (New York: Free Press, 1966), Chap. 9.
6. Charles W. Anderson, *Politics and Economic Change in Latin America* (Princeton, N.J.: Van Nostrand, 1967), p. 8.
7. Whitaker and Jordan, *op. cit.,* p. 14.
8. Quoted in Adams, *op. cit.,* p. 115.
9. The Generation of 1842 in Chile held similar views of the Spanish and of the past. See William R. Crawford, *A Century of Latin American Thought* (Cambridge, Mass.: Harvard University Press, 1961), Chap. 3.
10. For a more extensive discussion of the caudillo, see Hugh M. Hamill, *Dictatorship in Spanish America* (New York: Knopf, 1965).
11. Leopoldo Zea, *The Latin American Mind* (Norman: University of Oklahoma Press, 1963), p. 14.
12. Gerhard Masur, *Nationalism in Latin America* (New York: Macmillan, 1966), p. 32 ff.
13. For some interesting observations on racial mixture and

nationalism see Robert B. Toplin, "The Movement for Abolition of Slavery in Brazil: 1880–1888" (Ph.D. Thesis, Rutgers University, 1968).

14. Karl Deutsch, "Social Mobilization and Political Development," *American Political Science Review,* LV, No. 3 (September 1961), 493–514.

15. Crawford, *op. cit.,* p. 79 ff.

16. See E. Bradford Burns, *The Unwritten Alliance: Rio-Branco and Brazilian-American Relations* (New York: Columbia University Press, 1966).

17. José Ingenieros, *Sociología Argentina* (Buenos Aires: Ediciones L. J. Rosso, 1925), pp. 473–506.

18. The Haitians developed a concept of nationality based on race during this period. See Hans R. Schmidt, "The United States Occupation of Haiti: 1915–1934" (Ph.D. Thesis, Rutgers University, 1968), pp. 174–200, 311–312.

19. For example see José Angel Espinosa, *El ejemplo de Sonora* (Mexico: Gobierno de Sonora, 1932), and *Informe que el C. General de División Juan Andreu Almazán, Secretario de Communicaciones y Obras Públicas rinde al C. Presidente de la República con relación a su viaja por el noroeste del país* (Mexico, 1930), p. 33.

20. See Samuel L. Baily, *Labor, Nationalism and Politics in Argentina* (New Brunswick, N.J.: Rutgers University Press, 1967), pp. 51–70.

21. See Diego Rivera and Bertram Wolfe, *Portrait of America* (New York: Covici, Friede, 1934), p. 193.

22. See Alberto Methoe Ferre, *La izquierda nacional en la Argentina* (Buenos Aires: Editorial Coyoacan, 1963), and Leon Trotsky, *Por los Estados Unidos de América Latina* (Buenos Aires: Ediciones Coyoacan, 1961).

23. Jaguaribe and the other moderates resigned from the Institute in 1959 after a dispute with the radicals. The radicals then took charge and ran the Institute until it was abolished by the government of Castelo Branco in 1964.

24. For a study of this phenomenon in Argentina, see Marvin Goldwert, "The Argentine Revolution of 1930: The

Rise of Modern Militarism and Ultra-Nationalism in Argentina" (Ph.D. Thesis, University of Texas, 1961).

25. *Annals of the American Academy of Political and Social Science,* 334 (March 1961), pp. 3–6.

26. Carlton J. H. Hayes, *The Historical Evolution of Nationalism* (New York: Macmillan, 1931).

27. Whitaker and Jordan, *op. cit.,* pp. 14–15.

❧ I ❧

Nineteenth-Century
Latin America

1

Simón Bolívar

Proclamation to the People of Venezuela

In June 1812, Spanish forces defeated the Venezuelan patriot army at Puerto Cabello and imprisoned or exiled many of the creole or white native leaders. Simón Bolívar (1783–1830), who was to become the liberator of the northern portion of South America, went into exile on the island of Curaçao and then in New Granada. Early in 1813 he gathered together a small volunteer army and returned to Venezuela and declared a savage (and eventually successful) "war to the death" against the Spanish. On June 15, 1813, in the early stages of this effort, Bolívar addressed the people of the city of Trujillo and sought to win support for his cause. This speech is important because it clearly illustrates Bolívar's intense anti-Spanish feelings and his identification with a broad Americanism as well as with Venezuela.

Venezuelans: An army of your brothers, sent by the Sovereign Congress of New Granada, has come to liberate

---

From Vicente Lecuna and Harold A Bierck, eds., *Selected Writings of Bolívar* (New York: Colonial Press, 1951), I, 31–32. Printed by permission of the Banco de Venezuela.

you. Having expelled the oppressors from the provinces of Mérida and Trujillo, it is now among you.

We are sent to destroy the Spaniards, to protect the Americans, and to reëstablish the republican governments that once formed the Confederation of Venezuela. The states defended by our arms are again governed by their former constitutions and tribunals, in full enjoyment of their liberty and independence, for our mission is designed only to break the chains of servitude which still shackle some of our towns, and not to impose laws or exercise acts of dominion to which the rules of war might entitle us.

Moved by your misfortunes, we have been unable to observe with indifference the afflictions you were forced to experience by the barbarous Spaniards, who have ravished you, plundered you, and brought you death and destruction. They have violated the sacred rights of nations. They have broken the most solemn agreements and treaties. In fact, they have committed every manner of crime, reducing the Republic of Venezuela to the most frightful desolation. Justice therefore demands vengeance, and necessity compels us to exact it. Let the monsters who infest Colombian soil, who have drenched it in blood, be cast out forever; may their punishment be equal to the enormity of their perfidy, so that we may eradicate the stain of our ignominy and demonstrate to the nations of the world that the sons of America cannot be offended with impunity.

Despite our just resentment toward the iniquitous Spaniards, our magnanimous heart still commands us to open to them for the last time a path to reconciliation and friendship; they are invited to live peacefully among us, if they will abjure their crimes, honestly change their ways, and coöperate with us in destroying the intruding Spanish government and in the reëstablishment of the Republic of Venezuela.

Any Spaniard who does not, by every active and effective means, work against tyranny in behalf of this just cause, will be considered an enemy and punished; as a traitor to the nation, he will inevitably be shot by a firing squad. On the other hand, a general and absolute amnesty is granted to those who come over to our army with or without their arms, as well as to those who render aid to the good citizens who are endeavoring to throw off the yoke of tyranny. Army officers and civil magistrates who proclaim the government of Venezuela and join with us shall retain their posts and positions; in a word, those Spaniards who render outstanding service to the State shall be regarded and treated as Americans.

And you Americans who, by error or treachery, have been lured from the paths of justice, are informed that your brothers, deeply regretting the error of your ways, have pardoned you as we are profoundly convinced that you cannot be truly to blame, for only the blindness and ignorance in which you have been kept up to now by those responsible for your crimes could have induced you to commit them. Fear not the sword that comes to avenge you and to sever the ignoble ties with which your executioners have bound you to their own fate. You are hereby assured, with absolute impunity, of your honor, lives, and property. The single title, "Americans," shall be your safeguard and guarantee. Our arms have come to protect you, and they shall never be raised against a single one of you, our brothers.

This amnesty is extended even to the very traitors who most recently have committed felonious acts, and it shall be so religiously applied that no reason, cause, or pretext will be sufficient to oblige us to violate our offer, however extraordinary and extreme the occasion you may give to provoke our wrath.

Spaniards and Canary Islanders, you will die, though you be neutral, unless you actively espouse the cause of America's liberation. Americans, you will live, even if you have trespassed.

2

Januario da Cunha Barbosa

———◆▶◀◆———

Discourse Spoken at the Founding of the Brazilian Historical and Geographical Institute

Early in 1839, a number of Brazil's most distinguished intellectuals gathered in Rio de Janeiro to establish the famous Brazilian Historical and Geographical Institute. At this session Januario de Cunha Barbosa, the First Secretary of the organization, explained that the purpose of the Institute was to "eternalize the historical and memorable events of the Patria," and to offer this knowledge, "purified of errors," to the world. He reveals a mild anti-Portuguese feeling and a vague romantic sense of nation which characterized Brazilian nationalism throughout most of the nineteenth century.

It is no longer befitting to the Brazilian spirit, always conscious of the glory of the Patria, to leave unknown the notable events of her history as they occurred in various parts of the Empire. This, gentlemen, is the reason why two members of the council of the Society for the Aid of National Industry and several members of the Historical Institute of Paris, sharing the noble feelings of our men of

From *Revista do Instituto Histórico e Geográphico do Brazil,* I, No. 1 (1839), excerpts from pp. 10–21. Translated by the editor.

letters, undertook to propose the establishment of a Brazilian Historical and Geographical Institute. The reunification and organization of the facts of Brazilian history and geography will come about under the auspices of such a useful and respectable society. Notable historical events have occurred unrecorded throughout the various provinces, making it difficult for any patriot wishing to write precisely about our history to fulfill his task. The proposal to establish this Institute, as you all know, gentlemen, was crowned with success and general approval because of the patriotism and love of letters which animates the distinguished members of the Society for the Aid of National Industry.

We are assembled today to begin the work of the proposed Brazilian Historical and Geographical Institute, to show the cultured nations that we honor the glory of the Patria. As a literary association, we propose to concentrate on the various events of our history and to clearly describe the geographical characteristics of our country. In so doing, we present this knowledge to the world, purified of the errors and inexactitudes that blemish it in many national and foreign publications.

It is enough that we remember what Cicero said about history to understand the advantages of an Institute composed of men renowned for their scholarly and literary qualities. "History," writes the Roman philosopher, "is the testament of the times, the light of truth and the school of life." By this judicious doctrine we shall recognize the tasks of our own association, entrusted, as in other nations, with eternalizing the historical and memorable events of the Patria, rescuing them from the abyss of time, and separating them from the thick clouds of partiality, partisanship, and ignorance that sometimes obscure them. How well we know what infinite proof of this exists in the many works, chiefly foreign, that circulate in the world! Our silence, reprehensible with regard to material that so affects the honor of our country, permits historians to copy each other, thereby propagating many inaccuracies. These inaccuracies must be corrected immediately.

The heart of the true Brazilian patriot aches when he hears the distorted stories told about such contemporary events as our glorious independence. These events are still within our reach because scarcely sixteen years have passed since that memorable period when a promising empire in the New World was added to the ranks of the established nations. Already much has been forgotten. . . .

Our history, divided into ancient and modern periods, must be subdivided into various fields and eras so that it will become of greater interest to the wise investigators of the development of our civilization. No matter what one considers: the conquest of the fearless missionaries who drew so many people to worship the cross set up by Cabral on this continent; the cross that seemed to him to have come forth from the tomb of the sun; the military exploits that penetrated the continent's thick forests and that defended this prodigious and fortunate discovery against foreign enemies jealous of our good fortune; the wealth of our country's mines and woods, the products of its land and mountains, the grandeur of its rivers and bays, the variety and splendor of its plant life, the abundance and preciousness of its fruit, the astonishing variety of its animals; or, finally, the always mild climate that makes the sugar mill of our patricians so productive, in all of these we will find an inexhaustible treasure of honorable memories and interesting ideas, a treasure which must be shown to the world in its correct light.

There is no lack of writers who have devoted themselves to the task of recording many of these events for posterity. They have been read in all eras with appropriate admiration. But spread out as we are over the vast territory that is now Brazil—the seat of an imperial throne—these writers have written more histories of particular provinces than a general history which links facts with clearly stated criteria, with philosophical dedication, and with the pure light of truth. Ah, if only the many writings of illustrious Brazilians could be brought forth to public light or conserved in archives so that posterity could take advantage of them. Perhaps then we might realize in part the doctrine of Cicero that calls history "the testament of the times."

But to our disgrace, and to that of our patriotism, we have seen and continue to see how many good writers and their works have been lost. The ignorance or carelessness of the writers' heirs soon deliver them into the abyss of time. Their names survive for a time on their tombstones until even they disappear. Not only do the historical facts about where they were born disappear, but so do those facts about the places they honored by their glorious task.

The sorrowful fate that weighed upon us for over 300 years was not the least of the causes for this pitiful lack of publication on matters pertaining to the Patria. Not permitted to have a printing press anywhere in the colony, we were forced to beg the favors of the Portuguese. In times of absolutism this intolerable monopoly, the worst aspect of Portuguese administration, was extended to the writings of our men of letters. For this reason the writings of our men of letters died in private studies without seeing the publishers' stamp, or they were distorted to accommodate the monopolistic system. They were made to fit that system as water fits the container it fills. . . .

. . .

Forgive me, gentlemen, if in giving an exposition on the advantages which will emanate from the establishment of our Institute, I have kept more in mind the national glory —a glory which always makes my Brazilian heart beat—than the difficulties involved in the task upon which we are about to embark. This majestic edifice we are constructing has as its base both the love of country and the love of letters.

We shall not be less motivated by this love than those who in other nations have already established such a glorious and useful monument. Brazil keeps in the depth of its soil as well as in the hearts of its sons and sincere friends, precious treasures which must be used for honorable tasks. Without work, without persistence in the great enterprises, the glory which shines with the names of the servants of the Patria will never be obtained. Geography is the light of history, and history, bringing forth from oblivion the memories of the Patria, honors those who consecrate themselves by such hard work. Therefore, gentlemen, we should not become discouraged by the difficulty of our projects. Let us fix our eyes on the good of our patricians, on the glory of our nation, on our own honor. Let us always celebrate the anniversary of the Brazilian Historical and Geographical Institute of which we are the founders. And let us always present to the public articles worthy of attention because of the useful work which we shall perform.

Domingo F. Sarmiento

Civilization or Barbarism

*The nationalism of many of the leaders of nine-
teenth-century Latin America was directed toward developing their countries by Europeanizing them. The
classic statement of this position was that of the
Argentine educator and statesman, Domingo F. Sarmiento (1811–1888), who in 1845, while in exile in
Chile to escape the regime of Juan Manuel de Rosas,
wrote the book,* Life in the Argentine Republic in the
Days of the Tyrants. *Sarmiento associated civilization
with Europe and with the Argentine cities, and barbarism with the native gaucho and the areas outside
the cities. In the following selection from his famous
book, Sarmiento summarizes his thesis and describes
the Argentine Revolution of 1810, the war against
the cities and the savageness of the native gaucho.*

*This book had a tremendous impact on nationalists
throughout Latin America. Many since then have
challenged Sarmiento's dichotomy of civilization and
barbarism, but no one has been able to ignore it
(see Documents 8 and 15).*

From Domingo F. Sarmiento, *Life in the Argentine Republic in
the Days of the Tyrants: or Civilization and Barbarism,* translated
by Mrs. Horace Mann (New York: Hurd and Houghton, 1868),
pp. 54–62.

Before 1810, two distinct, rival, and incompatible forms of society, two differing kinds of civilization existed in the Argentine Republic: one being Spanish, European, and cultivated, the other barbarous, American, and almost wholly of native growth. The revolution which occurred in the cities acted only as the cause, the impulse, which set these two distinct forms of national existence face to face, and gave occasion for a contest between them, to be ended, after lasting many years, by the absorption of one into the other.

I have pointed out the normal form of association, or want of association, of the country people, a form worse, a thousand times, than that of the nomad tribe. I have described the artificial associations formed in idleness, and the sources of fame among the gauchos—bravery, daring, violence, and opposition to regular law, to the civil law, that is, of the city. These phenomena of social organization existed in 1810, and still exist, modified in many points, slowly changing in others, and yet untouched in several more. These foci, about which were gathered the brave, ignorant, free, and unemployed peasantry, were found by thousands through the country. The revolution of 1810 carried everywhere commotion and the sound of arms. Public life, previously wanting in this Arabico-Roman society, made its appearance in all the taverns, and the revolutionary movement finally brought about provincial, warlike associations, called *montoneras,* legitimate offspring of the tavern and the field, hostile to the city and to the army of revolutionary patriots. As events succeed each other, we shall see the provincial montoneras headed by their chiefs; the final triumph, in Facundo Quiroga, of the country over the cities throughout the land; and by their subjugation in spirit, government, and civilization, the final formation of the central consolidated despotic government of the landed proprietor, Don Juan Manuel Rosas, who applied the knife of the gaucho to the culture of Buenos Ayres, and destroyed the work of centuries—of civilization, law, and liberty.

. . .

I have been obliged to traverse the whole of the route hitherto pursued, in order to reach the point at which our drama begins. It is needless to consider at length the character, object, and end, of the Revolution of Independence.

They were the same throughout America, and sprang from the same source, namely, the progress of European ideas. South America pursued that course because all other nations were pursuing it. Books, events, and the impulses given by these, induced South America to take part in the movement imparted to France by North American demands for liberty, and to Spain by her own and by French writers. But what my object requires me to notice, is, that the revolution—except in its external symbolic independence of the king—was interesting and intelligible only to the Argentine cities, but foreign and unmeaning to the rural districts. Books, ideas, municipal spirit, courts, laws, statutes, education, all the points of contact and union existing between us and the people of Europe, were to be found in the cities, where there was a basis of organization, incomplete and comparatively evil, perhaps, for the very reason it was incomplete, and had not attained the elevation which it felt itself capable of reaching, but it entered into the revolution with enthusiasm. Outside the cities, the revolution was a problematical affair, and so far as shaking off the king's authority was shaking off judicial authority, it was acceptable. The pastoral districts could only regard the question from this point of view. Liberty, responsibility of power, and all the questions which the revolution was to solve, were foreign to their mode of life and to their needs. But they derived this advantage from the revolution, that it tended to confer an object and an occupation upon the excess of vital force, the presence of which among them has been pointed out, and was to add a boader base of union than that to which throughout the country districts the men daily resorted. These Spartan constitutions, that warlike nature hitherto ill-satisfied by the free use of the dagger, that Roman-like idleness which could only be exchanged for the activity of a battle-field, that utter impatience of judicial control, were all to have at last a fit sphere of action in the world.

Revolutionary movements then began in Buenos Ayres, and the call met with a decided response from all the interior cities. The pastoral districts became unsettled and joined in the movement. Tolerably disciplined armies were raised in Buenos Ayres to be sent to Upper Peru and Montevideo, where the Spanish forces under General Vigodet were stationed. General Rondeau laid siege to Montevideo with a disciplined army, and Artigas, a noted chieftain, took part in the siege with some thousands of gauchos. Artigas had been a formidable outlaw till 1804, when the civil authorities of Buenos Ayres succeeded in bringing him over and inducing him to undertake the duties of country commandant, as a supporter of the same authorities upon whom he had, till then, made war. If the reader has not forgotten the baqueano, and the general requisites of a country commandant, he will readily understand the character and feelings of Artigas. After a time, Artigas and his gauchos withdrew from General Rondeau, and began to make war upon him.

The latter's position was the same as Oribe's when he conducted the siege of Montevideo while taking care of another enemy at his rear. The only difference between the cases is that Artigas was hostile at once to patriots and royalists. It is not my purpose to determine with precision the causes or pretexts which occasioned this rupture, and I am as little disposed to apply to it any designation from the language of politics, for none such would be appropriate. When a nation engages in a revolution, it is begun by the conflict of two opposing interests, the revolutionary and the conservative; among us the names of patriots and royalists were applied to the corresponding parties. It is natural for the victors, after their triumph, to separate into moderate and extreme factions, one set wishing to carry out all the consequences of the revolution, while their opponents seek to restrain it within certain bounds. It is also characteristic of revolutions for the originally conquered party to renew its organization, and to find a means of success in the dissensions of its conquerors. But when one of the parties called to the aid of a revolution, immediately loses its connection with the others, forms a third entity, and shows hostility indiscriminately to both combatants (royalists and patriots), this detached party is heterogeneous, not having been conscious of existence until that time, the revolution having served to develop it and make it known.

This was the element set in motion by the renowned Artigas. It was a blind tool, but a tool full of life and of instincts hostile to European civilization and to all regular organization; opposed to monarchy as to republicanism, because both came from the city and possessed already order and reverence for authority. This tool was employed by the various parties, principally by that least revolutionary, in the civilized cities, until in the course of time the very men who had summoned it to their aid, yielded to it; and with them fell the city, its ideas, its literature, its colleges, its tribunals, its civilization!

This spontaneous movement of the pastoral districts was so ingenuous in its first manifestations, so full of genius and expression in its spirit and tendencies, that its adoption and baptism by the parties of the cities, with the political names which divided them, makes the sincerity of the latter appear in the most unfavorable light. The force which supported Artigas in Entre Rios, did the same for Lopez in Santa Fé, for Ibarra in Santiago, for Facundo in the Llanos. Its essence was individual action; its exclusive weapon, the horse; its stage, the vast pampas. The Bedouin hordes which in our day disturb the Algerian frontier by their war-cries and depredations, gives an exact idea of the Argentine montonera, which has been made use of by men of sagacity, as well as by noted desperadoes. In Africa, at the present day, there exists the same struggle between civilization and barbarism; the *goom* and the montonera are distinguished by the same characters, the same spirit, the same undisciplined strategy. Immense masses of horsemen wander in each case over the wilderness, offering battle to the disciplined forces of the cities, if they feel themselves the stronger party; dispersing in all directions like clouds of Cossacks, if the fight is even, to unite again and fall unexpectedly upon their sleeping foes, snatch away their horses, and kill their laggards and advanced parties. Ever at hand, but too much scattered to be successfully attacked, impotent in battle, but powerful and invincible in an extensive region, they finally decimate and overpower an organized force by means of skirmishes, surprises, fatigues, and privations.

The montonera, as it appeared under the command of Artigas in the early days of the Republic, already showed that character of brutal ferocity and the promise of a reign of terror, which it was reserved for the immortal bandit, the Buenos Ayres land-owner, to convert into a legislative system applied to a civilized society, and to present to the contemplation of Europe, to the shame and disgrace of America. Rosas invented nothing; his talent was only that of copying his predecessors and combining the brutal instincts of the ignorant masses into a coolly planned system.

The thongs made of Colonel Maciel's skin, and by command of Rosas converted into a pair of manacles, have been actually seen by foreign officials, an outrage not without its precedent, under the rule of Artigas and the other barbarous and Tartaric chiefs of the time. The montonera of Artigas *waistcoated* its enemies; that is, sewed them up in an envelope of raw hide, and left them in the fields in this condition.

The reader may imagine all the horrors of this slow death, and this horrible punishment was repeated in 1836, in the case of a colonel in the army. The infliction of death by cutting the throat with a knife instead of by shooting, is the result of the butcherly instinct which led Rosas to encourage cruelty, to give executions a more barbarous form which he thought would give pleasure to the assassins; in other words, he changed the legal punishments recognized by civil society, for others which he called American, and in the name of which he invited his fellow-Americans to come forward in his defense when the sufferings of Brazil, Paraguay, and

Uruguay invoked the aid of the European powers to assist in their liberation from the cannibal, who was even then overrunning them with his sanguinary hordes. It is impossible to maintain the calmness needed to investigate historic truth when we are forced to remember at every step that America and Europe have been so long successfully deluded by a system of assassination and cruelty, scarcely tolerated in the African provinces of Ashantee or Dahomey.

Such is the character presented by the montonera from its first appearance; a singular kind of warfare and civil polity, unprecedented except among the tribes of the Asiatic plains, and not to be confounded with the habits, ideas, and customs of the Argentine cities, which were, like all South American cities, a continuation of European civilization, and especially that of Spain.

The only explanation of the montonera is to be discovered by the examination of the society from which it proceeded. Artigas, the baqueano and outlaw, at war with the authorities of the city, but bought over as provincial commandant and chief of equestrian bands, presents a type reproduced with little change in each provincial commandant who came to be a partisan leader. Like all civil wars in which deep differences of education, belief, and motives divide the parties engaged in them, the internal warfare of the Argentine Republic was long and obstinate, until one of the elements of the strife was victorious. The Argentine Revolutionary War was twofold: 1st, a civilized warfare of the cities against Spain; 2d, a war against the cities on the part of the country chieftains with the view of shaking off all political subjection and satisfying their hatred of civilization. The cities overcame the Spaniards, and were in their turn overcome by the country districts. This is the explanation of the Argentine Revolution, the first shot of which was fired in 1810, and the last is still to be heard.

❧4❧

La Pasadita

In September of 1847, General Winfield Scott entered Mexico City in the final victorious stage of the Mexican-American War (1846–1848). This war, in which Mexico lost half her territory and was forced to endure the presence of foreign troops on her soil, stimulated intense and widespread hostility toward the United States. The following romance-corrido or folksong of 1847 suggests the importance of a foreign threat to the development of nationalism. It is a manifestation of nationalism in a genuinely popular genre. The Bella Unión mentioned in the song was a hotel in Mexico City where prostitutes, called Margaritas, and the soldiers of General Scott met and danced. Often the merriment extended to the balconies of the hotel and crowds gathered on the street outside to mock the soldiers, to applaud in jest, and to sing "La Pasadita." This anti-United States attitude and other nationalist sentiments were frequently expressed in

From Antonio García Cubas, *El libro de mis recuerdos* (México: Imprenta de Antonio García Cubas, 1904), pp. 439–441. Translated by the editor.

*the folksongs of Mexico and also in those of some of
the other Latin American countries.*[1]

Ah, my friends, I am going to tell you
what happened to me in this city.
The Yankees came and I risked throwing rocks at them
and in passing tra-la-la la-la.

Now the Margaritas speak English,
and they say: do you love me?
and the answer is: yes.
I [the Margaritas] understand what money means.
It is very good,
and in passing tra-la-la la-la.

Now the gringos at every opportunity eat cheeses
and donkey fodder.
They are jackasses, they dance the cancan,
and in passing tra-la-la la-la.

Only women [like the Margaritas] have the heart
to associate with that nation [the soldiers of the United
   States].
They [the Margaritas] say: come on. But it is false,
and in passing tra-la-la la-la.

One must see the big-footed gringos dance,
then the leather of their boots squeaks like mice.

---

[1] See Merle E. Simmons, *A Bibliography of the Romance and Related Forms in Spanish America* (Bloomington: University of Indiana Press, 1963) and *The Mexican Corrido as a Source for Interpretive Study of Modern Mexico (1870–1950)* (Bloomington: University of Indiana Press, 1957); Vicente T. Mendoza, *El corrido mexicano* (México: Fondo de Cultura Económica, 1954); and Frederick C. Turner, *The Dynamic of Mexican Nationalism* (Chapel Hill: University of North Carolina Press, 1968), pp. 282–287.

They look like the pigs of La Bella Unión,
and in passing tra-la-la la-la.

All these girls from La Bella Unión
dance very lively, they dance the rigadoon.
They look like ladies of great quality,
and in passing tra-la-la la-la.

Only men are to be trusted
because that which they do is not evil.
Like the cat, they are used to coaxing,
and in passing tra-la-la la-la.

The damned Yankees never stop saying,
that they will destroy this nation.
I say to them: No! It will never happen,
and in passing tra-la-la la-la.

If the Margaritas were made of cake,
how many Margaritas I would love to eat.
But they have nails and they know how to scratch,
and in passing tra-la-la la-la.

⤙5⤚

Lucas Alamán

——◆◆◆——

The Sicknesses from Which the Country Suffers

*Lucas Alamán (1792–1853), leader of the Mexican
Conservatives for most of the period from Independence until his death, believed that his country needed
a centralized system of government if it were to survive and prosper. In this section from his* History of
Mexico, *Alamán argues for the re-creation of the
Spanish system of government of the mid-eighteenth
century, praises the integrity and efficiency of the viceroys, urges a return to Christian morality, and recom-
mends a commission of from three to five persons to
reform the political system in accordance with his
ideas. He speaks of reestablishing the Mexicans' lost
national character and his reforms might well have
contributed to the development of nationalism. But
in mid-nineteenth century Mexico, the association of
centralism and nationalism with the Spanish colonial
system limited the Conservatives' appeal. It was
Benito Juárez and the Liberals who succeeded in
capturing the mantle of nationalism.*

From Lucas Alamán, *Historia de Méjico* (México: Imprenta de
J. M. Lara, 1852), Vol. V, excerpts from pp. 930–948. Translated
by the editor.

If one followed with care the series of events referred to in this second part of our history, he will be able to note that some of the defects from which the Mexican nation suffers are the result of the general course of things and of the spirit of the country, and are not easy to remedy with immediate measures. Just as the damage has developed gradually, so it must be remedied little by little as society profits from the mistakes of the past. Fortunately, these defects are no longer of such great importance. By imitating Europe we have created the problems ourselves, and they therefore can be resolved with the appropriate measures. If we are patient, it is still possible to avoid all of the mistakes and to gain all of the advantages of the experiences of the rest of the world.

Other defects from which we suffer are the result of our institutions. For the executive power, the problem lies in the feebleness of its actions and in the lack of effective protection for the citizens against the abuses of this same power. On the one hand, the executive power is weak in order to conform with the law. On the other hand, it is absolute in order to break it. As for the legislative power, the problem lies in its excessive functions and in the defective composition of the co-legislative bodies. The congress as it is now constituted is not only useless, but an impediment to the regular order of any government which might be able to fill the needs of the nation. Regarding the states, the problem lies in their excessive power and in their inequality. These defects must be remedied in conformity with the country's traditions; otherwise the reform will not be popular or permanent. We must not attempt to alter drastically all that exists, but instead we must conserve the best features of the present system and suppress only that which is prejudicial and harmful.

One of our strongest traditions, and one which has contributed much to the origin, reestablishment, and conservation of the federal system, is that of loyalty to the locality or what is called provincialism. Reduced to just and prudent limits, provincialism should produce good results; it encourages greater care in the administration of the particular interests of each area and each state, and it stimulates education and useful works of leisure and decoration. This fondness for the place where one is born or is settled or owns property is observable in those attempts at revolution in which respect for and loyalty to the ancient capital of the nation is asserted. Thus, in 1823, we saw Colima separating itself from Guadalajara in order to deal directly, as a territory of the federation, with the government of Mexico. The same situation occurred in Orizaba, Mazatlán, Aguascalientes and other areas, and still others are inclined toward the same action. If existing states broke up into their constituent departments or districts, it would be to the advantage of all the departments. This alone, with the extensive consequences that it would have, would be enough to bring the nation out of all the difficulties in which it finds itself, by establishing a simple, symmetric, uniform and not-difficult-to-obtain order in all areas.

Before explaining these points, I must say that this [organization] would not be new; it would be the re-establishment of the ancient system of the government of New Spain before the creation of the intendancies that later became states. The principle is such that we can make exceptions with respect to those states of small size and population—Chiapas, Nuevo León, Querétaro and Tabasco—which should not be further divided. In executing this reform, it would be possible to add a part of those states of greater size and number of inhabitants to others, and to make all states roughly equal. France did this when it divided the ancient states and provinces into departments, and this division has greatly benefited that country because it has kept in power all of the governments that have come to power since the national assembly. . . .

In this manner, we would establish a system—symmetrical and uniform in all areas, economical to run, conforming with the opinions and traditions that have created it—adequate for the nation's government. The principles of the federation would be preserved and strengthened. The government's actions would hardly be felt and would not be contradictory, and therefore they would be more effective. The action of the congresses and governments of the states would be reduced to distributing local benefits and improvements. The state would be a paternal authority, but it would not become oppressive, as has happened in some cases, creating hate, exciting discontent and provoking revolution. The proprietor class would take a larger part in public affairs because it would be in its self-interest to do so. When it understood that this system depends upon it, the proprietor class would pledge itself to guarantee the system's continued existence. This would give birth to public spirit, now completely absent, and would reestablish the lost national character. Mexicans would have a name to honor, a country to defend, and a government to respect, not because of the fear of punishment, but because of the benefits it dispenses, the honor it acquires and the consideration it merits.

In order to obtain these goals, it is not essential that power fall on men of great capacity. Honor and integrity are all that is necessary. The skill with which the viceroys governed is due to these qualities. During the past century, they brought New Spain out of the condition of disorder and decadence to which it had been reduced during the last reigns of the Hapsburgs. Not only did they solve all of the existing administrative problems, but they also anticipated future problems. The Duke of Linares (1711–1716), the Marquis of Casafuerte (1722–1734), Bucareli (1771–1779), Revilla Gigedo (1789–1794)—they had no other secret. Apodaca (1816–1821), without other means than these, reestablished the public finances in circumstances much more difficult than the present ones. Their principles were those of Christian morality, and when they served the king faithfully, their loyalty was based on the firm belief that in this manner they were also serving God. On the same basis was formed the respectable class of employees that aspired to be promoted only by fulfilling its obligations, and to whose zealousness and intelligence is owed the efficiency of the offices of government. Because they were men, they at times transgressed and abused their positions. But when these men were clearsighted, like the Duke of Linares to whom "the most rigorous review is that of the viceroy's judgement by the Divine Majesty," it was impossible for them to fall into the excesses to which those who did not have this conviction succumbed.

In light of the above, it would be a good thing to name a commission, not to exceed three to five individuals, charged with the task of establishing the nation. This commission would not be opposed because of the small number of its members, because, in the fiction of the representative system, one can be represented by five as well as by one hundred. In accordance with the general plan that it might propose, this commission would have the power to name all those it believes necessary for the organization of each of the branches of government. All of the authorities and offices of the Republic would be obliged to assist the commission and to give it whatever information and data might be necessary. By the end of a year, all of its work would be concluded. This is the only possible way to reorganize, completely and simultaneously, all of the branches of the administration. It must be recognized that the system might not succeed in all parts from the beginning, but the experience of time will point out the problems that cannot be prevented before putting a political system into practice. At the end of two years we could revise all of it, keeping in mind the observations that had been made about each of the parts, in order to amend and rectify those things which needed change. Congress could make those changes that the course of time demanded.

6

Emiro Kastos

Antioquia and Its Customs

Localism or provincialism was a stronger force in most of nineteenth-century Latin America than was nationalism. In this selection, first published in the July 20, 1858, edition of El Tiempo *of Bogotá, the noted Colombian writer-entrepreneur-politician Juan de Dios Restrepo (1823–1894), writing under the pseudonym Emiro Kastos, provides a good example of the kind of pride and feeling of attachment that was felt for the locality. He describes the virtues and strengths of the people of Antioquia, a mountainous region in the central highlands of Colombia whose major city is Medellín, and attacks the people of other regions of the country. It is interesting to note his attack on the laziness and immobility that he perceives in the Spanish character, and his praise of the man who works with his hands.*

The population of Antioquia is unquestionably the most vigorous, enterprising and energetic of the Granadine Confederation. The traveler who passes through these arid

---

From Emiro Kastos, *Artículos escojidos* (London: Juan M. Fonnegra, 1885), pp. 262–267. Translated by the editor.

mountains—with the rugged and abrupt nature which places almost insuperable difficulties in the way of communication, agriculture, commerce and industry—must admire the pastures filled with cattle, the comfortable and clean lodgings, the happy villages, and the populous cities, on the slopes, in the valleys, on the cliffs, in all regions. With the exception of the Medellín valley, which is not only agreeable and pleasing but of inexhaustible fertility, the hot and unhealthy shores of the great rivers, and some of the mountains of the towns of the South, the country is generally infertile and cultivation very difficult. Transportation is painful. The grama grass fields require a great deal of labor. To extract gold from the bottom of those precipitous and tumultuous rivers, or to break the rock of jasper and granite requires the labor of titans. A weak and feeble population would have succumbed before this unyielding land. But the people of Antioquia have not feared the difficulties of the rugged territory that was their lot. They have built houses on peaks high enough to make eagles dizzy; they have constructed roads across nearly perpendicular slopes; they have cultivated unhealthful valleys, and they have burrowed the mountains and gone down to the bottom of rivers in search of gold.

Wherever there is a mine, wherever there is a little land, the miner and the farmer accomplish marvels. The axe and the bar are the favorite tools of those strong arms. One of the most picturesque scenes to be found in those capricious and romantic mountains is to witness the felling of the ancient trees at the blow of the axe. We lack statistical data, but we are certain without fear of erring, that in the State of Antioquia the number of bushels of wood cut down each year is four times greater than in the rest of the Republic.

The man of the mountains has unique vices and virtues. On the one hand he is generally superstitious and fanatic, obstinate in his habits and slow to involve himself in social reform and progress. On the other hand he is sober, hardworking, economical and a lover of order, the family and the home. Rare are the people born in mild climates and especially favored regions who have conserved for long their dignity and independence. In the primitive cradles of the human race—on the banks of the Ganges, the Euphrates, the Indus, in the plains of Babylonia, in the enchanted valleys of Kashmir, in all those regions scented with roses, shaded by palm trees, where man from birth finds himself caressed by a loving nature—no energetic virtue develops in man. Doubly weakened, he bows before any fearless conqueror. But the Albanians, the Corsicans, and the Swiss—all mountain peoples—although surrounded by powerful nations, have always remained proud and independent. We salute, therefore, the mountains as the sacred homes of independence and liberty.

The inhabitant of the shores of the Magdalena, lying in his hammock, passes many hours of the day sleeping and doing nothing. When he is pricked by hunger he throws a net into the river and procures a delicious food. In the patio, pepper and chile grow spontaneously. With the *guarapo* (cane liquor), nectar for the *calentano* (lowlander), and the banana, ambrosia for all the world, he completes a feast of which the proletarians of Europe have not even dreamed. But this easy, abundant, lazy life enervates his faculties, brutalizes and degrades him. He is born, he vegetates, he dies and, like the animals in the forests, he passes through life without leaving any trace. Enterprising peoples and distinguished men have come forth from difficulties and struggle. Note that those who have inherited wealth, who upon being born find all the roads of life open to them, few times are of any use and generally are inept and poltroons. On the other hand, all the exalted personages who have taken strong initiative in industry, politics and letters have been brought up in the rugged school of difficulties and disgrace.

The energy and integrity of the character of the people of Antioquia is due in large part, therefore, to that harsh struggle that has been waged with nature.

But the prosperity and strength of that people is attributable to the purity of their customs and to the healthy and strong institution of the family. As in primitive societies, they do not know any other way of living. Even in the populous cities men not finding pleasures, society, theater— life foreign to no class—necessarily take refuge in the home. And he who does not live with his family does not live. . . .

In my article entitled "Mi Compadre Facundo" I sketched with all possible accuracy one of those domestic epics so common in Antioquia, in which a man alone, poor, without protectors or resources, goes out fearlessly in pursuit of fortune, and through his tenacity and valor acquires wealth and position.

Disassociating himself from the laziness and immobility characteristic of the Spanish race, the man of Antioquia loves to travel and he possesses an intense desire for activity. When the mines are exhausted and the lands barren, the whole population collects its work tools, its domestic belongings and emigrates in search of more fortunate regions. Sickness and misery are not accepted tranquilly either by the individual or by the people. All conform to this aphorism: "to live is to struggle." Today a great part of the population has abandoned its ancient home and has moved to the mountains of the South, where it has burst forth by magic from within the forests, towns and cities. In all the corners of the Republic there are natives of Antioquia. They take part in all types of industry, they are found on all the roads and they are the cosmopolitans of America.

In Antioquia they practice hospitality as amply as among primitive peoples. As in the tent of the Bedouin Arab, or in the house of the mufti Turk the guest in the house of the man of Antioquia is inviolable and sacred. Although he might be a criminal he is defended and respected. The traveler feels an undefinable pleasure upon arriving at one of these mountain houses, where the chickens are nibbling the grass, the cows are mooing in the corral, the garden is cultivated perfectly, and the patio is planted with flowers. The tidiness and cleanliness in all parts reveal that work, abundance, the family and the woman reign there. Then the pleasure increases as one sees the frank and hospitable reception he receives. In order to entertain you they will kill the fattest chicken, pick the best vegetables, and prepare the most comfortable bed. As in the tents of Isaac and Jacob, the Rebeccas of the family bring the water jug and towel and serve the meal with complete cordiality and gentility.

Some believe the people of Antioquia Bœotian, and accuse them in a whisper of being rude and incompetent. These charges are not true and I protest against them. The practical sense of business and industry are qualities characteristic of the people of Antioquia. In applied mechanics they are very skillful and the artisans of Medellín are the most intelligent in the Republic. In the city of Antioquia musicians and troubadours emerge spontaneously. The sentiments of beauty, literature and science have not spread very much in an isolated province where there is little education and where all time is absorbed by material demands and the struggle with an ungrateful nature. But we venture to cite some of our own names and to say that Antioquia has furnished, like any other section of the Republic, its contingent of notable men. . . .

◦§7§◦

Fenelón Zuviría

———◆❙◆———

Manifesto to the Argentine People

*Since the eighteenth century, the Rio de la Plata
basin—encompassing what is now Argentina, Uruguay, Paraguay, and part of Brazil—has often been
the arena of conflict.[1] In 1828, the British were instru-
mental in establishing Uruguay as a buffer state between feuding Argentina and Brazil. Nearly forty
years later, Argentina and Brazil joined one of two
contending political factions in Uruguay to defeat
the Paraguayan dictator Francisco Solano López (President from 1862 to 1870). In May of 1865, López captured the river port of Corrientes and led his army
across a section of Argentina to reach Uruguay. Argentina declared war on Paraguay and several days
later National Deputy Fenelón Zuviría, speaking in
behalf of his congressional colleagues, explained why*

From República Argentina, Cámara de Diputados de la Nación,
Diario de Sesiones, I, pp. 11–13 (May 10, 1865). Translated by the
editor.
[1] See Robert N. Burr, "The Balance of Power in Nineteenth-
Century South America: An Exploratory Essay," *Hispanic American Historical Review,* XXXV (1955), 37–60.

*war was necessary. His speech illustrates the impact of
a foreign threat on the development of nationalism.*[2]

When the Republic was resting quietly and enjoying the
advantages of peace and law which had been won with
half a century of bloody civil strife; when the period of
harmony had replaced that of destruction and hate; when
an enterprising internal policy and an essentially pacific
and neutral foreign policy had stimulated the development
of knowledge and had fomented many types of industry;
when all of these things had uplifted our image in the eyes
of other nations and had made us a refuge from civil and
political disgrace; it was then, without any provocation on
the part of the Republic and in complete disregard of the
protocol which use has converted into the law of nations,
that a man as uncautious as presumptious, heir to a dynastic
and somber presidency which rules over the most unfortunate people of America, perpetrated deceitful and barbarous acts against the honor, the existing pacts, and the
most sacred rights of the Republic.

The Argentine Government at the opening of Congress
informed us of the following: that the Paraguayan Government, without a previous declaration of war, violating the
faith of public treaties between the two countries, without
any provocation as well as without stated cause, sent a squadron of warships carrying infantry forces against the port of
Corrientes. With deceit and unheard-of treachery, the Paraguayans exchanged a flag salute with the anchored and
bedded warship, *25 de mayo,* and then opened fire on the
ship and captured it. The same thing happened to another
small naval ship which was being repaired. Following this,
the Paraguayans fired upon the defenseless population of
the city of Corrientes, and took both ships to Acunción.

After this deceitful deed, Paraguayan forces invaded the

---

[2] For the Paraguayan view of the war see Harris G. Warren,
"The Paraguayan Image of the War of the Triple Alliance,"
Americas, XIX (July 1962), 3–20.

city of Corrientes which, oblivious and peaceful, was un-armed and unable to resist or repel the Vandalic invasion.

Because of such crimes the Government asked Congress for the authority to declare war on the invader, and this authority was granted by instant and enthusiastic acclamation.

The Congress and the Government ardently desired peace and perpetual friendship with all nations. But outrages so serious and insulting to the dignity of a strong people —whose flags have waved as victoriously over the frozen crests of the Andes as under the strong rays of the equatorial sun—have compelled us to repel the act of force with force and to call the people to arms.

The people, in whose veins the enthusiasm has circulated with the speed of electricity and who are faithful to our glorious traditions, have come running to the call of the Patria. At this moment our ships loaded with soldiers are going up the rivers which lead to the somber den of the Paraguayan tyrant. The magnificent shores of the Paraná and the Uruguay reverberate with the presence of the children of Chacabuco and Maipú who, arm in arm, march to wash away the stain thrown upon the white and blue flag by the impure hand of a despot.

They also march to secure the liberty and human rights of an unfortunate people segregated from the American community. The Paraguayans are people of our blood, our language, our history and our religion, and they have not yet seen the majestic Sun of May rise in their land. It is decreed by God that liberty must be enthroned where the bicolored flag waves. The country that might become our enemy, observe carefully. Read about the love of the rights of men written in the pages of history with the generous blood of soldiers. The rights of men have always been preceded by the shining beacon of justice and honor, and followed by a reasonable and valiant people.

One is scarcely able to conceive of the senseless and deceitfully presumptuous deed of the Paraguayan oppressor. He provoked a nation unused to tolerating insults, a nation of a power superior to that of the short-lived despot. It is truth, revealed by philosophy and history, that in the long run Providence will produce results that favor humanity.

When Atila, at the head of seven hundred thousand Huns, was marching to surround a corrupted Rome, an unknown influence led him to continue, in happiness and ignorance, his mission. The primitive force of the rough children of the forest regenerated the abject slaves of the Caesars who were languishing in the lap of a refined and corrupt civilization.

Men without religion and believers in a vague ideal, marched unknowingly to destroy the temples of paganism —in which all the vices which dishonored humanity were being deified—and to build upon their ashes a monument to the cross, to liberty and to modern civilization.

López, by a contrary although equally rigorous logic, provoked the Republic, and thus is fulfilling the destiny that has marked this as the hour of the expiation and redemption of his country.

The Argentine people join in a cordial alliance with the Empire of Brazil and with Uruguay to fulfill the humanitarian mission of saving an enslaved people, an American pariah, and of moving it into the path of progress that until today was obstructed by an autocrat who wrapped himself in the mantle of democracy.

The flag of the Republic could no longer be mocked by its placement at the door of an uncivilized despot.

It was no longer possible to support the vibrating protest against American democracy and the progress of the century, personified in the Paraguayan Government. It was not possible to permit the continuation of this stain on the map of America in the beautiful region that surrounds the Paraguay and the Paraná Rivers.

It was not possible for us to tolerate—in grave danger to this country, to all the peoples of the Plata, and to humanity—the stupid prohibition to navigate the magnificent abundant waters that cross and fertilize one of the most plentiful territories of creation.

Citizens of the Republic, if with sufficient reason it was said that war is the worst of evils, it is also true that war is imperative and beneficial when the salvation of affronted honor and the triumph of principles that dignify and improve the human condition demand it.

Run then to take up arms—your cause is just. Quickly help your brothers, the brave sons of Corrientes, who alone and unprepared have contained the audacious invader.

Your mission is easy because you are going to fight unhappy people, exhausted by misery, and unified and motivated by terror. Theirs is the service of fearful slaves; it is not the valor of a soldier of honor and conviction. Because of this, our crusade will be glorious and magnificent both for the Patria and for democracy.

Run Argentines! Use your swords to cut a marital laurel branch in the virgin forests of Paraguay and offer it, after victory, as an olive branch of peace. Let this be a lesson of liberty to the innocent people who suffer in its shadow.

War to López! Liberty and love to the people of Paraguay!

◆8◆

José Martí

———◆◆◆———

Our America

Toward the end of the century a few men began to look within Latin America for the answer to their search for identity. One such person was the famous Cuban patriot José Martí (1853–1895). In this address to the Liberal Party of Mexico on January 30, 1891, Martí rejects the pervasive idea of Sarmiento that the important conflict in Latin America is between civilized Europeans and barbarous natives. He argues instead that Americans should look within and know their countries in order to govern them better. He insists that the Latin Americans cannot apply foreign solutions to their problems. The mestizo has conquered the foreign-dominated whites and he is the only one capable of liberating his country from all forms of tyranny.

In what Patria can a man have more pride than in our suffering American Republics, raised among the mute masses of Indians to the noise of the clash of book and *cirial* [reli-

From *Hispanoamérica en lucha por su independencia* (México: Cuadernos Americanos, 1962), pp. 115–117. Translated by the editor.

gious processional candleholder], over the bloody hands of a hundred apostles. Never, in recent history, have such progressive and unified nations been created out of elements so rotten. The arrogant man believes that because he has a facile pen or tongue, the earth is his pedestal. He accuses his native republic of incompetence and hopelessness because it does not give him the means with which to travel about the world as an important man, riding Arabian steeds and pouring champagne. The incapacity lies not with the nascent country—which seeks suitable models and effectual greatness—but rather with those who wish to govern primitive peoples of unique and violent composition with laws developed over four centuries of unencumbered practice in the United States and nineteen centuries of monarchy in France. A decree of Hamilton will not stop the charge of the *llanero's* horse. A phrase of Sieyés will not free the coagulated blood of the Indian race.

In order to govern well, one must pay attention to reality. The wise leader in America is not he who knows how the German or the Frenchman is governed, but he who knows of what elements his own country is composed and how he can guide them as a unity—by means of methods and institutions native to his own country—toward that desirable condition in which each man knows himself and exerts himself, and in which all men enjoy the abundance that Nature created for those who work for its fruitfulness and defend it with their lives. The government must be born of the country. The spirit of the government must be that of the country. The form of the government must adjust itself to the inherent structure of the country. Government is nothing more than the balance of the natural elements of the country.

For this reason, the imported book has been defeated by the native. The natural men have defeated the artificially erudite. The native mestizo has defeated the foreign creole. There is no struggle between civilization and barbarism, but rather between false erudition and nature. The natural man is good, he respects and rewards superior intelligence, but he will not permit it to endanger, offend or ignore him. That is the thing the natural man will not excuse; he is disposed to recover by force the respect of those who wound his pride or who prejudice his interest. The tyrants of America have risen to power through an affinity with the disdained natural elements. They have fallen when they have betrayed these elements. The Republics have been purged, by the tyrannies, of their inability to know the true elements of the country, of deriving from them the form of government, and of governing with them. Governor, in a new country, means creator.

In nations where there are cultured and uncultured groups, the uncultured will govern because of their custom of attacking and resolving doubts by force and because the cultured groups do not learn the art of government. The uncultured mass is lazy and timid in matters of intelligence, and it desires to be well governed. But if the government hurts it, this mass shakes off the government and governs itself. How can the universities produce leaders, if there are no universities in America where the rudiments of the art of government are taught—that is, the analysis of the unique features of the peoples of America? Uncertain, the young men go out into the world with Yankee or French spectacles, and they aspire to direct a people they do not know. In the political race access must be denied to those who do not know the rudiments of politics. The prize for the scholarly competitions does not have to be for the best ode, but for the best study of the elements of the country in which the author lives. It is essential—in the press, the university, the academy—to deal first with the real elements of the country. To know them thoroughly is enough, because a man who puts aside, purposely or accidentally, a part of the truth, will in the end fall under the weight of the truth he ignored. Ignored truth grows in negligence and overthrows that which rises without it. To resolve the problem once all of its elements are known is easier than to resolve it without knowing them.

The natural man comes, indignant and strong, and overturns the justice accumulated from books; it is not administered in accordance with the obvious necessities of the country. To know is to resolve. To know the country and to govern it on the basis of this knowledge is the only way to liberate it from tyranny. The European university must cede to the American university. The history of America from the Incas to the present must be taught in detail, even if one does not teach about the archons of Greece. Our Greece is preferable to the Greece which is not ours. Ours is more necessary. National politicians must replace foreign politicians. Graft the world onto our Republics, but the trunk must be that of our Republics. Silence the vanquished pedant. There is no Patria in which men can be more proud than in our suffering American Republics. . . .

❧9❧

John N. Plank

History and the Peruvian National Idea

The relationship of history and the past to national-
ism is important because nationalists can use or reject
the past as a basis upon which to build a nation. In
this selection, John N. Plank, Director of Political
Development Studies at the Brookings Institution in
Washington, raises several issues relating to history
and Peruvian nationalism. He challenges the state-
ment by the noted Peruvian Jorge Basadre in his book
Perú: problema y posibilidad, *that "history was the*
only factor that was capable of giving unity and sup-
port to the nation." Plank argues that Peruvians were
unable to use their past for the purposes of nation-
building because most Peruvians were illiterate and
knew little of the past, and because the literate Peru-
vians were hard pressed to find any "glory" in that
past.

Some years ago the Peruvian historian Dr. Basadre remarked,
". . . Everything that does not emanate from the historical

From John N. Plank, "Peru: A Study in the Problems of Nation
Forming" (Ph.D. Thesis, Harvard University, 1958), pp. 185–196.
Reprinted by permission of John N. Plank.

is, in Peru, radically heterogeneous." It was Dr. Basadre's contention that the Peruvian nation was a product of history which could be seen to be a nation only when viewed over a long historical perspective. Other factors in the Peruvian situation—race, language, geography, economy—were divisive and disruptive. History was the only factor that was capable of giving unity and support to the nation, the only factor that made legitimate the claim that Peru was a nation. We have seen enough in preceding chapters to be disposed to agree with Dr. Basadre that Peruvian society is indeed heterogeneous. Now we must examine his proposition that history is a unifying factor in the Peruvian context.

One may comment immediately that the history of Peru, whatever content individual historians may give it and whatever interpretations they may put upon that content, makes up almost no part of the intellectual baggage of the tremendous majority of those who live in Peru. Most who live in the state have never entered a school, have never read a printed word, have never attended a lecture. Of those who have received schooling, most have received too little to have acquired more than the most rudimentary notion of what Peru's history is and of its significance. The history of Peru, therefore, cannot be one of the links that bind them as individuals into membership in the Peruvian national community, for they do not know it nor do they meaningfully identify themselves with it.

Nevertheless, Peru's nation bearers legitimately stress the importance of history as an element of the national idea, and those responsible for drafting educational programs lay major emphasis upon the teaching of history, regarding such teaching as an effective means of instilling national awareness in the minds of the country's students.

A problem arises, however, in elaborating a history of Peru that will serve to awaken feelings of solidarity and pride among Peru's young citizens. Many Peruvians have pointed out that the history of republican Peru is anything but "glorious," being largely a sorry chronicle of political opportunism and corruption, economic shortsightedness and backwardness, social disunity and incoherence, and cultural mimesis and sterility. And, as Dr. Basadre has put it, "if history is going to dissociate, it is better not to teach it."

There are two aspects of the country's history that particularly concern us here. One is the "meaning" of that history, the other is the nature of Peru's "great men," its cultural heroes. The first is more important than the second, because cultural heroes can be manufactured pretty much *ad libitum* and can be unmade almost as easily, while tampering with the broad outlines of a country's history is difficult.

Bearers of the Peruvian nation are hard put to it to find meaning in Peru's history, or, at least, to find meaning that can serve as a focus of loyalties for most of those who live in the state. Throughout the colonial period Peru had been the center of Spanish power in South America, and it came to political independence in the face of the opposition of most of its leading *criollo* and *peninsular* inhabitants. Most of the rest of the population were utterly apathetic, caring little whether the masters of Peru were Spanish or Peruvian. Spanish resistance in Peru was crushed only after it had been completely eliminated elsewhere on the continent and only as a result of the intervention of troops from outside Peru under the leadership of the generals San Martín of Argentina and Bolívar of Gran Colombia. Among the comparative handful of Peruvian intellectuals and merchants who agitated for separation there was no consensus as to the form of government the new state ought to adopt, but there was general agreement that real economic and social revolution was to be abhorred. As a result, independence brought political anarchy, few significant changes in the economic and social spheres.

Peru produced not a single independence leader of the first rank, not a one who enjoys a reputation that carries beyond the frontiers of Peru. A number of its early presidents were turncoats, maverick soldiers who began their military careers fighting for the Spanish crown, then switched opportunely to the cause of independence when it appeared that their personal fortunes would be served thereby. Its intellectual leaders were wooly-minded theorists, much given to discussing Rousseau and to drafting unworkable constitutions, completely unprepared to assume the responsibilities of statesmanship, completely undisposed to work effectively for the implementation of the reforms they ostensibly espoused. An effort is being made today to resuscitate some of these dusty figures, to make of them cultural heroes in order that the Peruvian pantheon be respectably replete; and the effort can be applauded. But it has its pathetic aspect. Who is Unanue when contrasted with Colombia's Nariño? Who is Sánchez Carrión when contrasted with Argentina's Moreno? Who is Riva Agüero when contrasted with Rivadavia? And where are the Peruvian equivalents of Sarmiento, Alberdi, Echeverría? They do not exist. The fact that Peru has no equivalent of George Washington or Benjamin Franklin has its reasonable explanation, for there was nothing in Peruvian colonial society to succor Washingtons and Franklins. But the absence of such figures has worked a hardship on Peruvian nationalists who are attempting to structure a Peruvian nation.

Until well past mid-century political conditions within Peru were incredibly chaotic. Between 1821, when independence was declared, and 1857, Peru had thirty "presidents" of whom nineteen were "Generals" or "Marshals." Frequently the presidential office had two or more claimants simultaneously, and since orderly electoral procedures were unknown, the issue was resolved by the sword. During one incredible period in the 1840's there were seven "presidents" at once. The country seethed with local wars and lawlessness. Indeed, in 1837 Peru disappeared altogether as an independent state, it being federated with Bolivia under the dictatorship of Santa Cruz; and it did not reappear until 1839. How the history of this era can be rewritten so as to excite feelings of pride and national loyalty among young readers represents a grave challenge to Peru's nationalist historians.

The person Peruvian nationalists have chosen to eulogize

from this period is Ramón Castilla, a man of strong will if remarkably flaccid principle, who occupied the presidency from 1846 to 1851 and imposed a semblance of order upon the country. Castilla, a legitimate *caudillo,* is Peru's closest approximation to Argentina's extraordinary XIXth century figure Rosas, but he has never achieved the status of true folk hero that Rosas occupies.

Two events stand out in the history of Peru during the latter half of the XIXth century. One is the victory in 1866 of Peruvian shore batteries over a Spanish squadron of eleven ships that had threatened to blockade Callao: after an exchange of fire that endured less than eight hours, the Spanish ships withdrew. There were few casualties on either side, but a lucky hit by Spanish guns on a Peruvian observation point killed the Peruvian Minister of War, José Gálvez, who thereby found a place among Peru's warrior heroes.

The second event was the catastrophic defeat of the Peruvian forces by those of Chile in the War of the Pacific in 1879. As a result of this war, Peru lost its nitrate-rich regions in the south and was forced to endure the occupation of Lima by Chilean troops until 1884. Most Peruvian historians do not attempt to minimize the extent of this disaster or to conceal the political, economic and social rot in Peru that made it inevitable. But from the wreckage they salvage a handful of heroes whom school children can salute on appropriate dates and to whom monuments can be erected in the public plazas of Peru's principal cities. Admiral Grau and General Bolognesi are the most important. Both of them were vanquished by the Chileans, but not before they had led "glorious" harassing and delaying maneuvers.

There is little else in the history of the latter part of the XIXth century that can be utilized to bolster national pride. Politics remained the plaything of a tiny minority, the social and economic condition of the Indians and *cholos* continued to deteriorate, the output of Peru's intellectuals, both quantitative and qualitative, was insignificant.

What most forcibly strikes the student who examines the history of XIXth century Peru is that history's apparent meaninglessness. One finds in it few detectable trends, no concerted or coordinated drives toward recognizably Peruvian ends. There is nothing to correspond to the "Manifest Destiny" concept that determined much policy in the United States, nothing to correspond to the "Europeanization" of Argentine government and society. Instead, there is a welter of conflicting and incompatible currents, usually localistic, frequently individualistic, that collide and do not mesh, that sum to no positive result. The succession of events that attracts the attention of the student is kaleidoscopic, pyrotechnic, and as such moderately interesting; but it is not inspiring, not grand.

To be sure, during the XIXth century railroads were built—by the North American Henry Meiggs; steam navigation was introduced—by the North American William Wheelwright; new mines were brought into production—by North American, British and French interests. And to be sure, constantly in the background, passive and inarticulate, was the great mass of Indians and *cholos,* chained to the soil by tradition and economic necessity, quietly working, producing, breeding.

But what one finds nowhere in the history of the period is the spark of a "great idea" or the image of an indisputably "great man." Nothing identifiable as *peruanidad* emerged in Peru during the XIXth century.

The heritage of the XIXth century weighs heavily in the XXth. Today, as a hundred years ago, Peru is a congeries of incongruities. What "Peru" means, what in Peru's past is worth preserving, where Peru is going or ought to go— these are still unresolved questions. But in the XXth century, to a much greater extent than in the XIXth, they are alive and important questions that preoccupy a growing number of sensitive Peruvians. Until they are resolved, however, it will be difficult to give content to the intrinsically empty concept of *peruanidad* and difficult to educate young Peruvians to an awareness of the meaning and value of their national past.

10

Frederick C. Turner

Mestization and Class Differentiation

Racial unity and nationalism have often been closely linked in the minds of nationalists. In this selection, Frederick C. Turner, Associate Professor of Political Science at the University of Connecticut, points out that people can just as well associate the fusion of diverse races with nationalism. He illustrates that the dramatic increase in the proportion of mestizos in Mexican society during the nineteenth century was very important to the development of nationalism, because while the creole elites often identified themselves with Europe, and the Indians with the traditional locality, the mestizo identified himself and his self-interest with the emerging nation.

The composition and attitudes toward nationalism of Mexican classes and social groups shifted significantly in the

From Frederick C. Turner, *The Roots of Mexican Nationalism* (Ph.D. Thesis, Fletcher School of Law and Diplomacy, 1965), pp. 108–114. Reprinted by permission of Frederick C. Turner. The University of North Carolina Press has published a revised version of this dissertation under the title of *The Dynamic of Mexican Nationalism* (1968).

hundred years before 1910. Changes in the racial composition of the population through miscegenation brought changes in mestizo influence and attitudes, but of equal importance for the process of social integration were the comparatively stable attitudes of *criollo* and Indian groups. Besides attitudes in part traceable to a sense of race, the national allegiance of such diverse groups as illegitimate offspring and the members of the industrial sector of the economy also affected social integration.

The process of miscegenation or "mestization" by which the Indian and white races intermarried to form the mestizo group greatly changed the racial composition of Mexico during the XIXth century. In 1824 Humboldt estimated that 1,860,000 mestizos made up 27.3 percent of the Mexican population, while Ramón Beteta estimates that on the eve of the Revolution 8,000,000 mestizos made up 53 percent of the population. According to Humboldt and Beteta's figures, the number of white Mexican citizens fell from 1,230,000 in 1824 to 1,150,000 in 1910, and the proportion of white citizens fell from 18 percent of the total population to only 7.5 percent. Although the number of Indians rose from approximately 3.7 million to 6 million, the Indian proportion of the population fell from 54.4 percent to 39 percent. Even if we accept Ramón Beteta's opinion that a larger number of Mexicans were mestizos in the early XIXth century, the proportion of mestizos still rose from 38 percent to 53 percent in the hundred years before 1910. The biological mestization of the Mexican population was a gradual and irreversible process, because not only the union of whites and Indians but also that of mestizos with either of the other groups produces mestizo offspring. The length which the process had reached by 1910 is evident in the contemporary statement of Frederick Starr, an anthropologist from the University of Chicago, that "in some parts of Mexico, it almost seems as if what white-blood once existed is now breeded out."

In the early XIXth century when mestizos were still numerically inferior, they lacked both power and prestige.

Leopoldo Zea notes the early XIXth century rootlessness of the mestizos when he writes that they "surged to life accidentally, they were the unsought sons of whites and Indians. Neither one nor the other wanted them. . . . They were simple and pure *accidents* and as such had no place in colonial society." They lacked both the security of the *criollo* in being the legitimate heirs of their fathers and the paternal protection which the white Spaniard was obliged to offer to the Indian. The mestizo group contributed soldiers to the Army, trusted servants in city and country, and carried on most trades and manual arts. Nevertheless, the mestizo could not be master of a guild, take holy orders, carry arms or obtain political employment, while mestizo women were forbidden to wear gold ornaments, pearls or silks.

In trying to improve their own positions, mestizos came to champion the idea of a national community. Increasingly in the XIXth century mestizos took command of Mexico and used appeals to common Mexican nationality to legitimize their own place in society. Mestizos wanted to change the basis of economic and social advancement from ascription to achievement, to eliminate race and inherited social position as criteria for the acquisition of status. The steady rise in the number of mestizos as well as their drive to gain status through achievement increased their power within Mexican society.

Mexicans came to associate the process of mestization with the formation of their national community, as writers like Andrés Molina Enríquez before 1910 emphasized the mestizo's role in national affairs. In 1915 Manuel Barranco claimed optimistically that "in a homogenous race, the consciousness of kind is strong, the feeling of nationality is powerful, and democracy is possible." The new pride in the mestizo race comes out strongly in José Vasconcelos' 1925 study of *La raza cósmica*. Reiterating a common theme of Mexican educators, Octavio Vejar Vázquez later wrote that the "unity of a people is reached, in its highest and purest form, if the common spirit enters into the individual soul and on the biological plane the homogeneity of the blood of its members is achieved." Carlos Chávez has even defined Mexican music as mestizo music, writing that the "new music of Mexico, that is, *mestizo* music, the fruit of the two races and the two cultures put into contact by the Conquest, is very rich and varied." Associating mestization with a growing equality of opportunity for citizens of all racial backgrounds, Mexicans proclaim that all citizens should be "incorporated into the nationality economically as well as spiritually" in order to aid the process of mestization to break down the "artificial and antipatriotic barriers to national unity."

The process of mestization partly overcame the lack of racial homogeneity which worked against Mexican nationalism in 1810. Although the gradation of colonial classes resulted from intermarriage, the very process of intermarriage tended toward the classes' ultimate dissolution. As the *criollos* prided themselves on their European value system and most Indians were too geographically and culturally isolated to acquire national values, the mestizos developed a new pride in "Mexican" things. With their mixed blood they could not feel secure in the isolation of either the criollo or the Indian. Cultural mestization accompanied biological mestization, and other racial groups became increasingly aware of mestizo attitudes.

In taking national pride in the fusion of races, Mexicans in one sense differ widely from other nations where allegations of racial unity are a unifying force. A frequent aspect of nationalism is a belief in common origin which is often mistakenly conceived to be racial in nature. Mexicans were patently not of common origin, and the rise of nationalism among them demonstrates just how unnecessary is any common racial base. Just as the Swiss prove [the (unnecessariness) of common language], so the Mexicans have proved that a viable national group may be created from antagonistic races. In demonstrating the lack of need for racial unity, however, the Mexicans also prove that nationalism is effectively promoted by the fusion of races and appeals to the superiority of the new race which is thus formed.

Mestization also removed the underlying complementarity of Mexico's races which, together with their superficial antagonism, retarded the rise of nationalism. Despite the Conquest and subsequent racial friction, an element of truth lies in the notion that the Spaniard needs an Indian to be Spanish just as the Indian needs a Spaniard to be Indian. The Spaniard could acquire a proper sense of *dignidad* when he had someone like the Indian under him to do the ordinary, manual work which he rejected, so leaving him free for less mundane feats such as conquest or jousting against intellectual inertia. Before the Conquest most Mexican Indians lived in highly stratified societies, so that Spanish subjugation reinforced their inherited cultural patterns. The proportion of the Mexican population which either as Spaniards or Indians could derive their sense of identity from being "above" or "below" steadily declined, however, with the process of mestization.

❧ II ❧

Twentieth-Century
Latin America

A) 1900–1930

‹❧ 11 ❧›

Euclides da Cunha

———◆►◆◄◆———

Rebellion in the Backlands

In the 1890s, Antônio Conselheiro, a primitive mystic, gathered a flock of faithful in the small town of Canudos in the interior of the Brazilian northeast. The people of Canudos became involved in a series of clashes, then military campaigns, with the state and federal governments. By October 5, 1897, they were completely defeated. At the time, many believed that the Canudos uprising was a plot to restore the recently overturned monarchy (1889). In 1902, Euclides da Cunha, who as a reporter for a São Paulo newspaper accompanied the final government expedition against Canudos, wrote Rebellion in the Backlands *and suggested a more profound meaning to the campaign. Canudos, he argued, manifested the disunity of Brazilian society; it was a conflict between the people of the backlands (sertão) and the civilization of the coast. Da Cunha is important because he publicized*

From Euclides da Cunha, *Rebellion in the Backlands*, translated by Samuel Putnam (Chicago: University of Chicago Press, 1964), pp. xxix–xxx, 161–163. Reprinted by permission of The University of Chicago Press. Copyright 1944. Copyright under International Copyright Union by the University of Chicago.

> *the people of the* sertão, *called for their inclusion in
> the national community, and linked nativism with
> social justice.*

Written in the rare intervals of leisure afforded by an active
and tiring life, this book, which originally set out to be a
history of the Canudos Campaign, subsequently lost its
timeliness when, for reasons which need not be mentioned
here, its publication was deferred. We have accordingly
given it another form, the theme which was the dominant
one in the beginning and which inspired the work being
now little more than a variation on the general subject here
treated.

It is our purpose to sketch in, however inadequately, for
the gaze of future historians, the most significant present-
day characteristics of the subraces to be found in the backlands of Brazil. We do this for the reason that the instability
of the multiple factors and diverse combinations that go to
make up this ethnic complex, together with the vicissitudes
of history and the lamentable lack of mental enlightenment
which prevails among them, is likely to render these races
short-lived, destined soon to disappear before the growing
exigencies of civilization and the intensive material competition offered by the stream of immigrants that is already
beginning to invade our land with profound effect. The
fearless *jagunço,* the ingenuous *tabaréo,* and the stolid
caipira are types that will soon be relegated to the realm of
evanescent or extinct traditions.*

The first effects of various ethnic crossings are, it may be,
initially adapted to the formation of a great race; there is

---

* The glossary at the back of the book gives the following definitions of these terms: caipira—countryman, rustic, of southern
Brazil; jagunço—this word, originally meaning a ruffian, in da
Cunha comes to be practically synonymous with *sertanejo,* or
inhabitant of the backlands; tabaréo—originally, an awkward,
clumsy military recruit; comes to have a general sense of rustic
or backwoodsman.

lacking, however, a state of rest and equilibrium, which the acquired velocity of the march of the peoples in this century no longer permits. Backward races today, tomorrow these types will be wholly extinguished. Civilization is destined to continue its advance in the backlands, impelled by that implacable "motive force of history" which Gumplowicz, better than Hobbes, with a stroke of genius, descried in the inevitable crushing of weak races by the strong.

The Canudos Campaign has, therefore, the undeniable significance of a first assault in a struggle that may be a long one. Nor is there any reason to modify this assertion in view of the fact that it was we, the sons of the same soil, who staged this campaign; inasmuch as, being ethnologically undefined, without uniform national traditions, living parasitically on the brink of the Atlantic in accordance with those principles of civilization which have been elaborated in Europe, and fitted out by German industry, we played in this action the singular role of unconscious mercenaries. What is more, these extraordinary native sons, living in a prevalent disunity upon a land that was in part unknown to them, are wholly separated from us by a co-ordinate of history—time.

.   .   .

The war of Canudos marked an ebb, a backward flow, in our history. What we had to face here was the unlooked-for resurrection, under arms, of an old society, a dead society, galvanized into life by a madman. We were not acquainted with this society; it was not possible for us to have been acquainted with it. The adventurers of the seventeenth century, it is true, would encounter in it conditions with which they were familiar, just as the visionaries of the Middle Ages would be at home among the *demonopaths* of Varzenis or the Stundists of Russia; for these epidemic psychoses make their appearance in all ages and in all places, as obvious anachronisms, inevitable contrasts in the uneven evolution of the peoples—contrasts which become especially evident at a time when a broad movement is vigorously impelling the backward peoples toward a higher and civilized way of life. We then behold the exaggerated Perfectionists breaking through the triumphant industrialism of North America, or the somber *Stürmisch* sect, inexplicably inspired by the genius of Klopstock, sharing the cradle of the German renascence.

With us, the phenomenon is perhaps still more readily to be explained. After having lived for four hundred years on a vast stretch of seaboard, where we enjoyed the reflections of civilized life, we suddenly came into an unlooked-for inheritance in the form of the Republic. Caught up in the sweep of modern ideas, we abruptly mounted the ladder, leaving behind us in their centuries-old semidarkness a third of our people in the heart of our country. Deluded by a civilization which came to us second hand; rejecting, blind copyists that we were, all that was best in the organic codes of other nations, and shunning, in our revolutionary zeal, the slightest compromise with the exigencies of our own national interests, we merely succeeded in deepening the contrast between our mode of life and that of our rude native sons, who were more alien to us in this land of ours than were the immigrants who came from Europe. For it was not an ocean which separated us from them but three whole centuries.

And when, through our own undeniable lack of foresight, we permitted a nucleus of maniacs to form among them, we failed to see the deeper meaning of the event. Instead, we looked at it from the narrow-minded point of view of partisan politics. In the presence of these monstrous aberrations, we had a revealing fit of consternation; and, with an intrepidity that was worthy of a better cause, we proceeded to put them down with bayonets, thereby causing history to repeat itself, as we made yet another inglorious incursion into these unfortunate regions, opening up once more the grass-grown trails of the bandeiras.

In the backlands agitator, whose revolt was a phase of rebellion against the natural order of things, we beheld a serious adversary, a mighty foeman representing a regime which we had done away with, one who was capable of overthrowing our nascent institutions.

And Canudos was our Vendée.

In the last days of the settlement, when it was permitted them to enter what was left of the huts, the conquerors found a grievous disappointment awaiting them. Their hard-won victory gave them the right to sack these ruined homes, and nothing was exempt from their insatiable curiosity; but it was one of the most unremunerative bits of pillaging that history has to record. In place of rich spoils, they found mutilated images and cocoanut-shell rosaries; but what most excited their covetousness was the scrawled documents, and especially the terrible verses which they discovered among the latter. Poor bedraggled sheets of paper on which the barbarous orthography paralleled the most naïve absurdities, while the irregular and unsightly handwriting seemed to be a photographic reproduction of the twisted way of thinking of these people; it appeared to sum up the psychology behind the conflict. These scraps of paper were worth everything in the world for the reason that they were worth precisely nothing. On them the sermons of Antonio Conselheiro were written down; and, as one read them over, one realized just how innocuous his preachings really were after all, reflecting simply the poor fellow's intellectual turmoil. Every line of them was vibrant with the same vague and incongruous religiosity, but there was very little of political significance to be found in any one of them, such as might have lent itself to the messianic tendencies revealed. If the rebel attacked the established order, it was because he believed that the promised kingdom of bliss was near at hand. He denounced the Republic as a mortal sin on the part of the people, the supreme heresy, heralding the ephemeral triumph of the Anti-Christ. And these rude poets had put his hallucinations into the form of colorless rhymes; for they lacked the strongly marked spontaneity of the backlands improvisers. Nevertheless, in these foolish verses they left us living documents; and, as we read them, we could not but agree with Renan that there is a rude and eloquent second Bible of the human race to be met with in the stammerings of the people.

❧ 12 ❧

Manuel Ugarte

The Only Patria

In the decades following the Spanish American War, many Latin Americans attacked the growing influence of the United States in Latin America. These attacks often generated a defensive nationalism. One such critic was the Argentine Manual Ugarte (1878–1951), who in La Patria grande, Mi campaña hispanoameri-cana, El porvenir de América Latina, *and* El destino de un continente—*all written between 1910 and 1917 —argued and reiterated his case. In this selection from* El porvenir de América Latina, *first published in 1910, Ugarte attacks United States imperialism and argues that the only way to prevent the subjugation of all Latin America by the Anglo-Saxon powers is to create one great Latin American nation, conscious of its distinct Hispanic origins and traditions, and prepared to defend its independent future. His argument for continental nationalism and his explanation of the relationship of the more traditional forms of nationalism to continental nationalism influenced*

From Manuel Egarte, *El porvenir de América Latina* (Buenos Aires: Editorial Indoamérica, 1953), pp. 112–118. Translated by the editor.

many other Latin American intellectuals, particularly those who joined such movements as Acción Ibero-americana and the Unión Latinoamericana which developed during the 1920s. Although continental nationalism seems to be quite different from the other forms of the phenomenon, Ugarte illustrates its importance for some.

Latin Americans cannot help saying: "In the immense territories to the North, another race dominates in all the splendor of its genius. Its strength grows greater every minute. Its ambition has no limits. It is like an ocean covering the plains. Mexico has lost various provinces. Cuba is smothering under a painful protectorate. The customs houses of Santo Domingo do not exist. The Panama Canal absorbs Central America. Money strangles the smallest republics and no one knows before what river or mountain this assault by a country whose population growth demands an indefinite expansion will stop. Already the Yankee has made us suspect what he is doing. Nothing will stop him from reducing our size if his happiness demands it. Perhaps he wishes to conceal his desire to extend his domination like an expanding ocean. But shall we shut our eyes in order not to see the future? Will we, concentrating on our childish vanities, abandon ourselves to the melancholy of watching the rise of the ocean that will submerge us? Is the absorption of the Latins by the Anglo-Saxons inevitable? Will we submit to this fate? Shall we passively accept the 'land-grabbing' and the policy of the 'big-stick?' Instead of uniting to avert the landslide, shall we continue multiplying our differences? Shall we awake to the danger only when it has crushed us?"

An Anglo-Saxon recently said: "Because of the Panama Canal, Central America will soon be in the same position, with respect to the United States, that Cuba has been for some time." Let us not blame the assault on anyone but ourselves.

What has handicapped us until now has been our notion of nationality. Our frontiers are broader than what is commonly assumed by those who only pay attention to maintaining ephemeral domination. They do not comprehend that what is more important than the interests of the group are those of the Patria, and that what is more important than those of the Patria are those of the moral confederation which the Latins form within the continent.

Paul Leroy Beaulieu set down three conditions for the preservation of our common independence: order within the states, peace among the sister republics, and economic relations with Europe. In order not to continue aiding the Yankees, it is most urgent to establish a loyal relationship among the parties within the nation and among the nations within our threatened America. Above our struggles floats something like a superior preoccupation, a spirit of race, an ultimate patriotism that is the result of all the others. At least in what is called international politics, we should have one Patria, and we might be able to defend it in the highest manner—with the sacrifice of egotistic passions, subordinating local interests to the salvation of the whole.

The future depends on us. "Progress will come about if we want it to," said Tarde, "if we are aware of its qualities and means, and if we judge it by subordinating our desire to our spirit of sacrifice. If we only believe it will come about, it will not." Thus it is with the salvation of Latin America. It will be the result of our perseverance, of our disinterestedness, or it will not be.

We have already seen that the association of republics is not a wild dream. Italy was formed with heterogeneous provinces and Germany united principalities that fought more than once. Nothing obstructs the rapprochement of countries born of the same revolution and the same ideal. Let us suppose that in a great Latin American assembly, after admitting the urgency of eliminating the rivalries that weaken us, it is resolved to give practical form to the desire for union that is in the atmosphere. Let us imagine it is agreed that each of the twenty republics name delegates, and that, without interfering with internal administration, those representatives establish themselves as a Committee of Foreign Relations and assume the superior direction and external representation of the race. They would confine themselves exclusively to our façade before the world, in accordance with the general laws discussed in the respective parliaments. Which country could feel itself threatened? The central organ that would place our pride and our territorial integrity above all greediness would guarantee the independence of the adhering countries rather than diminish it. By obstructing interventions, the central organ would leave all in a better position to fulfill, within the limits of each state, the ideals of local democracy.

Only those of little importance would oppose the realization of the project. But reaching this point, nothing would be easier than to calm them, giving the small nations representation which would balance the predominance of the others, and specifying that the committee would operate successively in each of the capitals, moving according to alphabetical order, number of inhabitants, or the day on which they proclaimed independence. In any case, the details of implementation must not place obstacles in the way of the triumph of an idea comprehended and adopted by all, especially in a case in which the fact of wanting the *entente* is equivalent to consenting to the sacrifices without which it is impossible.

The creation of a supreme means to coordinate the pulses of the race, to give the necessary cohesion to our eighty million people who must face the future struggles, and to present one block, one will, and one formula before the foreigner—this would finally dissipate the doubts which delay the transformation of the project into reality. We should not let ourselves be convinced by those who call a dream everything which has not already taken place. The future is not an illusion, but unexpressed life that waits for the right moment to come forth. We can bring forth this life with a flex of the muscles. To fulfill their destinies and maintain their vigor, nations need something like that which maintains the freshness of lakes; a stream of pure water that carries enlivening germs, and a continuous drain to remove the useless elements. We must know how to forget the elements that maintain our tradition, in order to favor the triumph of renovating energies which await to become manifest. We must familiarize ourselves with the impossibilities because in the majority of cases they alone are evident. When the will to conquer is alive, the drive to fulfill is always stronger than the resistance to it.

By diminishing the distance between the republics, we will defend to the depths the spirit which animates us. It is not only the independence of a people that is to be saved, but also a civilization now beginning to define itself. The soul of the race is reborn in the New World and the Latins of America have the duty to preserve that which is born of them. Like the Latins of Europe, the Latins of America feel the obligation to provide the appropriate setting for what might become the brilliant extension of a Latin hegemony. Let us extirpate the infantile opinion that the danger does not exist. Let us destroy the discouraging belief that the situation is hopeless. The creative impulse to reconstruct the future is paralyzed by the empty optimism of some and by the resigned pessimism of others. We should remember at all times, that the men who brought about independence— such as [Simón] Bolívar and [José de] San Martín—always had a propensity toward union. The disintegration, with the passions and the factions, came later. Past are the periods of disorientation and delirium that were perhaps necessary because—like the plow that destroys in preparation for future harvests—they appealed to the continental conscience. It is just that the propensities of the founders of the Patria arise again. The redeeming energy might force us toward what appears to be unobtainable. The first attempts at agreement will take shape under the spur of danger, developing into an alliance which might be the first step toward the triumphal confederation.

From the moral point of view we already form a firm block. What difference is there between Chilean, Uruguayan, Venezuelan and Peruvian literature? With slight variations, one observes from North to South only one spirit.

As to institutions, have not all of us adopted the republic, and are we not proud of the same qualities and critical of the same defects of the republic? As to language, the essential bond among groups, do we not conserve the cult which the mother country bequeathed us? Are not our heroes in many cases the same? Upon encountering in Europe a Latin American born in the republic farthest from ours, do we not respond to some obscure impulse that makes us consider him as a resident of our own native city? And does not the Spanish blood and the American sap that jumbles us under one denomination circulate equally in our veins?

Let us have faith in the future. The notion of the greatness of tomorrow is strengthened by the growing gains of national pride; the impetus is encouraged with the help of a conviction; horizons are enlarged by the urgency of uniting the Patrias; Latin America can aspire to the highest and most lasting triumphs. Everything contributes to making Latin America one of the summits of the world. Its privileged position, which affords it every type of climate from Ecuador to the southern sea; its unlikely prosperity which places it at the head of the exporting nations; its virile youth, its generous cosmopolitanism, and its noble audacity —all of these things transform it into a field open to the promises of the sun. If prudence places it under the protection of mortal supervision, one could say that the species has won a field of gold. We are not suggesting substituting one selfish ruler for another, or of stopping Anglo-Saxon tyranny in order to impose our own. Our concern is to maintain the free play of a nationality internationally fed, and to open in the world the possibility of action under the protection of Latin civilization.

Let us tear down the obstacle to our success. America is today like those games which consist of an infinite number of concentric boxes; one breaks through the first and the second appears; one destroys the second and the third presents itself. Each time there is further division which seems to be the work of maniacs determined to pulverize life. The moment of synthesis has arrived. The duty to lead the crusade belongs to Argentina, Brazil, Chile and Mexico. The prestige, the culture and the progress of these countries enables them to resolve the situation. From the collective point of view, dispersion hurts us more than daily defeat. From the particular point of view, each country finds itself indefensible before the threat of imperialism. We need not concern ourselves with what our contemporaries may say, but rather with that which the future will judge. The best patriots will be those who subordinate local to continental patriotism.

To preserve ourselves from the assault of the Yankees, we must do what a divided and anarchic Argentina did fifty years ago in order to defend itself from a brother nation like Brazil. The Panama Canal modifies world perspectives and our great cities of the South, oriented partially toward the practical idealism which predominates among the Anglo-Saxons, must now lead the crusade, pitting the victorious civilization that flowers on the coasts of the Atlantic against the aggressive covetousness of the new conquerors.

❧13❧

Mexican Constitution of 1917, Article 27

Article 27 of the Mexican Constitution of 1917 is one of the basic documents of popular nationalisms all over Latin America because it subordinates private property rights to those of the nation and thus provides a justification for land reform and expropriation of natural resources. It declares that the Mexican nation is the original owner of all land, water and natural resources within the boundaries of the national territory, and that private property is created only when the nation transmits title to private persons. If private property is created only by concession of the nation, it can also be taken away from its individual owner if the nation should need it. In addition, this article sets forth rules to protect the communal land, to determine who may own property, and to establish the uses of the land.

From *Constitution of the United Mexican States: 1917* (Washington: Pan American Union, 1967), pp. 8–15.

Article 27. Ownership of the lands and waters within the boundaries of the national territory is vested originally in the Nation, which has had, and has, the right to transmit title thereof to private persons, thereby constituting private property.

Private property shall not be expropriated except for reasons of public use and subject to payment of indemnity.

The Nation shall at all times have the right to impose on private property such limitations as the public interest may demand, as well as the right to regulate the utilization of natural resources which are susceptible of appropriation, in order to conserve them and to ensure a more equitable distribution of public wealth. With this end in view, necessary measures shall be taken to divide up large landed estates; to develop small landed holdings in operation; to create new agricultural centers, with necessary lands and waters; to encourage agriculture in general and to prevent the destruction of natural resources, and to protect property from damage to the detriment of society. Centers of population which at present either have no lands or water or which do not possess them in sufficient quantities for the needs of their inhabitants, shall be entitled to grants thereof, which shall be taken from adjacent properties, the rights of small landed holdings in operation being respected at all times.

In the Nation is vested the direct ownership of all natural resources of the continental shelf and the submarine shelf of the islands; of all minerals or substances, which in veins, ledges, masses or ore pockets, form deposits of a nature distinct from the components of the earth itself, such as the minerals from which industrial metals and metalloids are extracted; deposits of precious stones, rock-salt and the deposits of salt formed by sea water; products derived from the decomposition of rocks, when subterranean works are required for their extraction; mineral or organic deposits of materials susceptible of utilization as fertilizers; solid mineral fuels; petroleum and all solid, liquid, and gaseous hydrocarbons; and the space above the national territory to the extent and within the terms fixed by international law.[1]

In the Nation is likewise vested the ownership of the waters of the territorial seas, within the limits and terms fixed by international law; inland marine waters; those of lagoons and estuaries permanently or intermittently connected with the sea; those of natural, inland lakes which are directly connected with streams having a constant flow; those of rivers and their direct or indirect tributaries from the point in their source where the first permanent, intermittent, or torrential waters begin, to their mouth in the sea, or a lake, lagoon, or estuary forming a part of the public domain; those of constant or intermittent streams and their direct or indirect tributaries, whenever the bed of the stream, throughout the whole or a part of its length, serves as a boundary of the national territory or of two federal divisions, or if it flows from one federal division to another or crosses the boundary line of the Republic; those of lakes, lagoons, or estuaries whose basins, zones, or shores are crossed by the boundary lines of two or more divisions or by the boundary line of the Republic and a neighboring country or when the shoreline serves as the boundary between two federal divisions or of the Republic and a neighboring country; those of springs that issue from beaches, maritime areas, the beds, basins, or shores of lakes, lagoons, or estuaries in the national domain; and waters extracted from mines and the channels, beds, or shores of interior lakes and streams in an area fixed by law. Underground waters may be brought to the surface by artificial works and utilized by the surface owner, but if the public interest so requires or use by others is affected, the Federal Executive may regulate its extraction and utilization, and even establish prohibited areas, the same as may be done with other waters in the public domain. Any other waters not included in the foregoing enumeration shall be considered an inte-

---

[1] As amended by decree published in the Diario Oficial of January 20, 1960.

gral part of the property through which they flow or in which they are deposited, but if they are located in two or more properties, their utilization shall be deemed a matter of public use, and shall be subject to laws enacted by the States.[2]

In those cases to which the two preceding paragraphs refer, ownership by the Nation is inalienable and imprescriptible, and the exploitation, use, or appropriation of the resources concerned, by private persons or by companies organized according to Mexican laws, may not be undertaken except through concessions granted by the Federal Executive, in accordance with rules and conditions established by law. The legal rules relating to the working or exploitation of the minerals and substances referred to in the fourth paragraph shall govern the execution and proofs of what is carried out or should be carried out after they go into effect, independent of the date of granting the concessions, and their nonobservance will be grounds for cancellation thereof. The Federal Government has the power to establish national reserves and to abolish them. The declarations pertaining thereto shall be made by the Executive in those cases and conditions prescribed by law. In the case of petroleum, and solid, liquid, or gaseous hydrocarbons no concessions or contracts will be granted nor may those that have been granted continue, and the Nation shall carry out the exploitation of these products, in accordance with the provisions indicated in the respective regulatory law.[3]

It is exclusively a function of the general Nation to conduct, transform, distribute, and supply electric power which is to be used for public service. No concessions for this purpose will be granted to private persons and the Nation will make use of the property and natural resources which are

---

[2] As amended on November 9, 1940, and by decree published in the Diario Oficial of January 20, 1960.

[3] As amended by decree published in the Diaro Oficial of January 20, 1960.

required for these ends.[4] (Note: A transitory provision of the amendment adding the foregoing paragraph to Article 27 states:

"A regulatory law shall establish the rules to which concessions granted prior to the enactment of the present law (amendment) shall be subject.")

Legal capacity to acquire ownership of lands and waters of the Nation shall be governed by the following provisions:

I. Only Mexicans by birth or naturalization and Mexican companies have the right to acquire ownership of lands, waters, and their appurtenances, or to obtain concessions for the exploitation of mines or of waters. The State may grant the same right to foreigners, provided they agree before the Ministry of Foreign Relations to consider themselves as nationals in respect to such property, and bind themselves not to invoke the protection of their governments in matters relating thereto; under penalty, in case of noncompliance with this agreement, of forfeiture of the property acquired to the Nation. Under no circumstances may foreigners acquire direct ownership of lands or waters within a zone of one hundred kilometers along the frontiers and of fifty kilometers along the shores of the country.[5]

The State, in accordance with its internal public interests and with principles of reciprocity, may in the discretion of the Secretariat of Foreign Affairs authorize foreign states to acquire, at the permanent sites of the Federal Powers, private ownership of real property necessary for the direct services of their embassies or legations.[6]

II. Religious institutions known as churches, regardless of creed, may in no case acquire, hold, or administer real property or hold mortgages thereon; such property held at present either directly or through an intermediary shall revert to the Nation, any person whosoever being authorized

---

[4] Paragraph added by decree of December 23, published in the Diario Oficial of December 29, 1960.

[5] See n. 3.

[6] Paragraph added on November 9, 1940.

to denounce any property so held. Presumptive evidence shall be sufficient to declare the denunciation well founded. Places of public worship are the property of the Nation, as represented by the Federal Government, which shall determine which of them may continue to be devoted to their present purposes. Bishoprics, rectories, seminaries, asylums, and schools belonging to religious orders, convents, or any other buildings built or intended for the administration, propagation, or teaching of a religious creed shall at once become the property of the Nation by inherent right, to be used exclusively for the public services of the Federal or State Governments, within their respective jurisdictions. All places of public worship hereafter erected shall be the property of the Nation.

III. Public or private charitable institutions for the rendering of assistance to the needy, for scientific research, the diffusion of knowledge, mutual aid to members, or for any other lawful purpose, may not acquire more real property than actually needed for their purpose and immediately and directly devoted thereto; but they may acquire, hold, or administer mortgages on real property provided the term thereof does not exceed ten years. Under no circumstances may institutions of this kind be under the patronage, direction, administration, charge, or supervision of religious orders or institutions, or of ministers of any religious sect or of their followers, even though the former or the latter may not be in active service.

IV. Commercial stock companies may not acquire, hold, or administer rural properties. Companies of this kind that are organized to operate any manufacturing, mining, or petroleum industry or for any other purpose that is not agricultural, may acquire, hold, or administer lands only of an area that is strictly necessary for their buildings or services, and this area shall be fixed in each particular case by the Federal or State Executive.

V. Banks duly authorized to operate in accordance with the laws on credit institutions may hold mortgages on urban and rural property in conformity with the provisions of such laws but they may not own or administer more real property than is actually necessary for their direct purpose.

VI. With the exception of the corporate entities referred to in clauses III, IV, and V hereof, and the centers of population which by law or in fact possess a communal status or centers that have received grants or restitutions or have been organized as centers of agricultural population, no other civil corporate entity may hold or administer real property or hold mortgages thereon, with the sole exception of the buildings intended immediately and directly for the purpose of the institution. The States, the Federal District, and the Territories, and all Municipalities in the Republic, shall have full legal capacity to acquire and hold all the real property needed to render public services.

The federal and state laws, within their respective jurisdictions, shall determine in what cases the occupation of private property shall be considered to be of public utility; and in accordance with such laws, the administrative authorities shall issue the respective declaration. The amount fixed as compensation for the expropriated property shall be based on the value recorded in assessment or tax offices for tax purposes, whether this value had been declared by the owner or tacitly accepted by him by having paid taxes on that basis. The increased or decreased value of such private property due to improvements or depreciation which occurred after such assessment is the only portion of the value that shall be subject to the decision of experts and judicial proceedings. This same procedure shall be followed in the case of property whose value is not recorded in the tax offices.

The exercise of actions pertaining to the Nation by virtue of the provisions of this article shall be made effective by judicial procedure, but during these proceedings and by order of the proper courts, which must render a decision within a maximum of one month, the administrative authorities shall proceed without delay to occupy, administer, auction, or sell the lands and waters in question and all their appurtenances, and in no case may the acts of such authorities be set aside until a final decision has been rendered.

VII.[7] The centers of population which, by law or in fact, possess a communal status shall have legal capacity to enjoy common posession of the lands, forests, and waters belonging to them or which have been or may be restored to them.

All questions, regardless of their origin, concerning the boundaries of communal lands, which are now pending or that may arise hereafter between two or more centers of population, are matters of federal jurisdiction. The Federal Executive shall take cognizance of such controversies and propose a solution to the interested parties. If the latter agree thereto, the proposal of the Executive shall take full effect as a final decision and shall be irrevocable; should they not be in conformity, the party or parties may appeal to the Supreme Court of Justice of the Nation, without prejudice to immediate enforcement of the presidential proposal.

The law shall specify the brief procedure to which the settling of such controversies shall conform.

VIII. The following are declared null and void:

a) All transfers of the lands, waters, and forests of villages, *rancherias,* groups, or communities made by local officials (*jefes politicos*), state governors, or other local authorities in violation of the provisions of the Law of June 25, 1856, and other related laws and rulings.

b) All concessions, deals or sales of lands, waters, and forests made by the Secretariat of Development, the Secretariat of Finance, or any other federal authority from December 1, 1876 to date, which encroach upon or illegally occupy communal lands (ejidos), lands allotted in common, or lands of any other kind belonging to villages, *rancherias,* groups or communities, and centers of population.

c) All survey or demarcation-of-boundary proceedings, transfers, alienations, or auction sales effected during the

---

[7] Amended by decree dated November 24, 1937 and published in the Diario Oficial of December 6, 1937.

period of time referred to in the preceding sub-clause, by companies, judges, or other federal or state authorities entailing encroachments on or illegal occupation of the lands, waters, or forests of communal holdings (ejidos), lands held in common, or other holdings belonging to centers of population.

The sole exception to the aforesaid nullification shall be the lands to which title has been granted in allotments made in conformity with the Law of June 25, 1856, held by persons in their own name for more than ten years and having an area of not more than fifty hectares.

IX. Divisions or allotments of land among the inhabitants of a given center of population which, although apparently legitimate are not so, due to a mistake or defect, may be annulled at the request of three fourths of the residents holding one fourth so divided, or one fourth of such residents holding three fourths of the lands.

X. Centers of population which lack communal lands (ejidos) or which are unable to have them restored to them due to lack of titles, impossibility of identification, or because they had been legally transferred, shall be granted sufficient lands and waters to constitute them, in accordance with the needs of the population; but in no case shall they fail to be granted the area needed, and for this purpose the land needed shall be expropriated, at the expense of the Federal Government, to be taken from lands adjoining the villages in question.

The area or individual unit of the grant shall hereafter be not less than ten hectares of moist or irrigated land, or in default of such land its equivalent in other types of land in accordance with the third paragraph of section XV of this article.[8]

XI. For the purpose of carrying out the provisions of this article and of regulating laws that may be enacted, the following are established:

---

[8] This paragraph added on February 12, 1947.

a) A direct agency of the Federal Executive entrusted with the application and enforcement of the agrarian laws;

b) An advisory board composed of five persons to be appointed by the President of the Republic and who shall perform the functions specified in the organic laws:

c) A mixed commission composed of an equal number of representatives of the Federal Government, the local governments, and a representative of the peasants, to be appointed in the manner set forth in the respective regulating law, to function in each State, Territory, and the Federal District, with the powers and duties set forth in the organic and regulatory laws;

d) Private executive committees for each of the centers of population that are concerned with agrarian cases;

e) A communal office (comisariado ejidal) for each of the centers of population that possess communal lands (ejidos).

XII. Petitions for a restitution or grant of lands or waters shall be submitted directly to the state and territorial governors.

The governors shall refer the petitions to the mixed commissions, which shall study the cases during a fixed period of time and render a report; the State governors shall approve or modify the report of the mixed commission and issue orders that immediate possession be given to areas which they deem proper. The case shall then be turned over to the Federal Executive for decision.

Whenever the governors fail to comply with the provisions of the preceding paragraph, within the peremptory period of time fixed by law, the report of the mixed commission shall be deemed rejected and the case shall be referred immediately to the Federal Executive.

Inversely, whenever a mixed commission fails to render a report during the peremptory time limit, the Governor shall be empowered to grant possession of the area of land he deems appropriate.

XIII. The agency of the Executive and the Agrarian Advisory Board shall report on the approval, rectification, or modification of the reports submitted by the mixed commissions, containing the changes made therein by the local governments, and so notify the President of the Republic, who as the supreme agrarian authority will render a decision.

XIV. Landowners affected by decisions granting or restoring communal lands and waters to villages, or who may be affected by future decisions, shall have no ordinary legal right or recourse and cannot institute *amparo* proceedings.

Persons affected by such decisions shall have solely the right to apply to the Federal Government for payment of the corresponding indemnity. This right must be exercised by the interested parties within one year counting from the date of publication of the respective resolution in the *Diario Oficial*. After this period has elapsed, no claim is admissible.

Owners or occupants of agricultural or stockraising properties in operation who have been issued or to whom there may be issued in the future certificates of non-affectability may institute amparo proceedings against any illegal deprivation or agrarian claims on their lands or water.[9]

XV.[10] The mixed commissions, the local governments and any other authorities charged with agrarian proceedings cannot in any case affect small agricultural or livestock properties in operation and they shall incur liability for violations of the Constitution if they make grants which affect them.

Small agricultural property is that which does not exceed one hundred hectares of first-class moist or irrigated land or its equivalent in other classes of land, under cultivation.

To determine this equivalence one hectare of irrigated land shall be computed as two hectares of seasonal land; as four of good quality pasturage (agostadero) and as eight as *monte* (scrub land) or arid pasturage.

Also to be considered as small holdings are areas not exceeding two hundred hectares of seasonal lands or pasturage susceptible of cultivation; or one hundred fifty hectares of

---

[9] As amended on February 12, 1947.
[10] See n. 9.

land used for cotton growing if irrigated from fluvial canals or by pumping; or three hundred, under cultivation, when used for growing bananas, sugar cane, coffee, henequen, rubber, coconuts, grapes, olives, quinine, vanilla, cacao, or fruit trees.

Small holdings for stockraising are lands not exceeding the area necessary to maintain up to five hundred head of cattle (ganado mayor) or their equivalent in smaller animals (ganado menor—sheep, goats, pigs) under provisions of law, in accordance with the forage capacity of the lands.

Whenever, due to irrigation or drainage works or any other works executed by the owners or occupants of a small holding to whom a certificate of non-affectability has been issued, the quality of the land is improved for agricultural or stockraising operations, such holding shall not be subject to agrarian appropriation even if, by virtue of the improvements made, the maximums indicated in this section are lowered, provided that the requirements fixed by law are met.

XVI. Lands which are subject to individual adjudication must be partitioned precisely at the time the presidential order is executed, according to regulatory laws.

XVII. The Federal Congress and the State Legislature, within their respective jurisdictions, shall enact laws to fix the maximum area of rural property, and to carry out the subdivision of the excess lands, in accordance with the following bases:

a) In each State, Territory, or the Federal District, there shall be fixed a maximum area of land of which a single individual or legally constituted society may be the owner.

b) The excess over the fixed area shall be subdivided by the owner within the time fixed by the local law, and these parcels shall be offered for sale under terms approved by the governments, in accordance with the aforementioned laws.

c) If the owner should oppose the subdivision, it shall be carried out by the local government, by expropriation.

d) The value of the parcels shall be paid by annual

installments which will amortize principal and interest, at an interest rate not exceeding 3% per annum.

e) Owners shall be required to receive bonds of the local Agrarian Debt to guarantee payment for the property expropriated. For this purpose, the Federal Congress shall enact a law empowering the States to create their Agrarian Debt.

f) No subdivision can be sanctioned which fails to satisfy the agrarian needs of neighboring settlements (poblados inmediatos). Whenever subdivision projects are to be executed, the agrarian claims must be settled within a fixed period.

g) Local laws shall organize the family patrimony, determining what property shall constitute it, on the basis that it shall be inalienable and shall not be subject to attachment or encumbrance of any kind.

XVIII. All contracts and concessions made by former Governments since the year 1876, which have resulted in the monopolization of lands, waters, and natural resources of the Nation, by a single person or company, are declared subject to revision, and the Executive of the Union is empowered to declare them void whenever they involve serious prejudice to the public interest.

❧14❧

Frederick B. Pike

———◆●◆———

The Rise of Economic Nationalism in Chile, 1892-1920

In this selection, Frederick B. Pike, Professor of History at the University of Notre Dame, documents the rapid United States economic penetration of Chile during the early years of this century, and the Chilean response to this penetration. His discussion of the growth of economic nationalism as a political issue after 1910 illustrates one very important use of nationalism in Latin America.

Especially in the later years of the 1892–1920 period, distress over the economic penetration of the northern master-capitalist nation contributed to Chile's frequent manifestations of anti-United States sentiments. A brief glance at statistics reveals why this would be so, for the increasing importance of United States trade and investments to the Chilean economy, most particularly after 1910, is indeed striking.

In 1896, the total value of goods exchanged between Chile and the United States was slightly less than $3,000,000. In

From Frederick B. Pike, *Chile and the United States, 1880–1962* (Notre Dame, Ind.: University of Notre Dame Press, 1963), pp. 159–163. Reprinted by permission of the University of Notre Dame Press.

both exports and imports, the United States occupied fourth place in Chilean commerce, behind England, Germany, and France, in that order. Two years later Frank G. Carpenter, a Yankee journalist who traveled through Chile, commented upon the insignificance of United States trade and capital in the Chilean economic structure. Outside of Grace Company operations—the company had established its Valparaíso office in 1881 and a Santiago branch in 1885—Carpenter could find only one large-scale operation owned by Yankee interests. This was the silver mining and refining "kingdom" of New York capitalist George Chace. The owner of several of the richest silver mines in northern Chile, Chace also operated a profitable silver and copper refining plant in Iquique.

The Chilean commercial picture had changed by 1910. At that time the United States absorbed about $22,650,000 worth of Chilean exports—80 percent of this was represented by nitrates—virtually the same amount as Germany. The United Kingdom was still in first place by a considerable margin, buying over $40,000,000 worth of Chilean products, but France had ceased to be an important purchaser. In the same year Chile bought $12,271,000 worth of goods from the United States, $32,035,000 from the United Kingdom, $24,035,000 from Germany, and $6,434,000 from France. By 1913, Chile's export-import figures with the United States, Germany and the United Kingdom had all increased slightly, but the relative position of the three countries was unaltered. The First World War drastically transformed the Chilean commercial structure, eliminating Germany and propelling the United States far ahead of Great Britain. In 1920, Chilean exports to the United States were valued at $115,803,000, and imports reached $47,000,-000—figures that represented 54 percent of Chile's entire foreign trade. In contrast, the value of exports to the United Kingdom was $55,000,000, while imports were $39,160,000.

The increase of direct United States investments in Chile was also striking. Although in 1912 these investments totaled scarcely more than $15,000,000, the next eight years witnessed a remarkable upsurge. The Guggenheim interests, already by 1912 the owners of the rich copper mine of El Teniente, located in Sewell in central Chile, shortly later acquired the fabulous Chuquicamata mine in the north. After investing over $1,000,000 in the mine, the Guggenheim-controlled Chile Exploration Company began actual production at Chuquicamata in mid-May 1915, employing some 3,500 workers. Beginning also in 1915, Bethlehem Steel undertook the extraction of northern Chile's iron ore and within four years had exported 143,000 metric tons. By 1916 Grace and Company had offices in nine Chilean cities, and the National City Bank of New York had established a branch in Santiago. As the decade of the 1920's began, direct United States investment in mining, industry, and commerce in Chile had soared to over $250,000,000, while loans and portfolio investments amounted to an additional $100,000,-000. At this time, approximately one third of all United States private funds directly or indirectly committed to Latin America were invested in Chile.

To Chileans this fact did not represent an unmixed blessing. The presence of United States-financed operations in the country produced inevitable friction. By 1920 charges were being voiced in the Chilean Congress that United States copper firms imposed subhuman working conditions on their unfortunate laborers. Other United States operations were accused of controlling the votes of their employees, thereby securing election of "puppets" to the national Congress. More important, influential Chileans were becoming convinced that the United States was bent upon obtaining economic control over Chile as well as the rest of Latin America, and was using the Pan-American movement to accomplish this end. *El Mercurio* summed up this attitude: "In the Chilean Congress and in other informed circles, the prevailing opinion is that Pan-Americanism represents merely a materialistic attempt on the part of the United States to gain economic mastery over Latin America." Chilean suspicions of United States intentions, especially of Wilson's apparent desire to have United States

capital replace that of Europe in Latin America, were point-
edly expressed at the Buenos Aires Financial Conference
held in 1916. At the opening session of the conference, to
which the United States had sent a distinguished delegation
headed by Secretary of the Treasury William Gibbs Mc-
Adoo, Chilean representative Armando Quesada Acharán
proclaimed: "Closer economic ties between the United
States and Latin America must not, in any way, interfere
with the maintaining and increasing of economic relations
with Europe." And as the First World War came to an end,
Chileans became obsessed with the economic menace posed
by the United States, fearing that the Yankees might initiate
a dumping policy which would wipe out the recent gains
scored by domestic industry. In this respect, Eliodoro
Yáñez asserted that Chile was threatened by a calamity
worse than international war.

It is significant that economic nationalism was not introduced as a major issue into Chilean politics until sometime
after 1910, precisely the period in which United States economic influence first became apparent. An early, half-
hearted attempt of President Balmaceda to rally Chileans
against the peril posed by British economic pre-eminence
had won only a handful of supporters. But the new efforts,
directed against the United States, won a considerable following. Many of Chile's most respectable citizens were attracted to the Nationalist Union (*Unión Nacionalista*).
Founded in 1913, this organization was led by such promi-
nent men as Francisco Antonio Encina, the distinguished
upper-class historian-essayist, and Guillermo Subercaseaux,
perhaps the most renowned Chilean economist and banker
in the first third of the twentieth century. The Nationalist
Union, which briefly transformed itself into a political party
in 1915, attempted to bring an "economic and sociological
orientation" to Chilean politics. In particular, it urged nationalization of foreign-controlled industries and greater
governmental economic planning.

Other signs heralded the birth of economic nationalism
in Chile. Santiago in 1917 witnessed an imposing ceremony

honoring Argentina's prolific and fiery lecturer Manuel Ugarte, one of the most outspoken Yankeephobes ever to arise in Latin America. Upon this occasion both Marcial Martínez and Eliodoro Yáñez agreed that warnings of the Argentine writer against United States imperialism were now more timely than ever, in view of the new Yankee commercial invasion. About this time, Chileans also shuddered at the implications of a story told by the eminent journalist Trancredo Pinochet Le-Brun. While in New York, Pinochet claimed to have met a Spaniard who wanted to go to Chile to raise chickens, but who insisted postponing his departure until he had become a United States citizen. When queried as to this decision, the Spaniard explained: "If I am a United States citizen and someone steals chickens from me in Chile, the fleet will be sent to my aid."

Far and away the most significant point raised by the champions of economic nationalism was the assertion that foreign dominance of the national economy was an unmistakable sign of Chilean decadence and inferiority. The underlying contention here was that if Chile ever wished to become a modern republic, it must develop the technical skills and habits of industry for which it had heretofore relied upon foreigners. Francisco Antonio Encina made this point in his classic *Nuestra inferioridad económico*. Trancredo Pinochet had the same thing in mind when he urged Chileans to study in the United States in order to acquire technological proficiency. To allow Yankees to come to Chile to introduce advanced scientific methods would only result in greater United States dominance of Chile's economy. However, once well-trained Chileans returned from the United States, they would be able to stir their laggard compatriots into exercising their latent talents. Thus, Chileans would begin to develop their country by their own efforts. With this process once initiated, it would be possible to oust the foreigners. But if Chileans refused to follow this policy, he warned, "then we will remain a fossilized reminder of a bygone age, or else become the subjects of more economically advanced nations."

❧15❧

Ricardo Rojas

From Eurindia

The Argentine writer Ricardo Rojas (1882–1957)
was a leading cultural nationalist in Latin America.
In his books La restauración nacionalista *(1909),*
Blasón de plata *(1910), and* La argentinidad *(1916),*
he argues that Argentina had to develop a collective
conscience based on her own traditions, and par-
ticularly on those native traditions of the interior.
He rejected Sarmiento's dichotomy between civiliza-
tion and barbarism and instead claimed that the
struggle was between indianism (nativism) and ex-
oticism (foreign influence). The following selection
from Eurindia, *published in 1922, indicates that*
Rojas had changed his mind somewhat; he argued
for a synthesis of foreign and native elements. Latin
America, he suggests, needs exoticism to develop po-
litically, and indianism to develop its cultural tradi-
tions.

From Ricardo Rojas, *Eurindia* (Buenos Aires: Editorial Losada,
1951), pp. 15–21. Translated by the editor. Permission granted by
Carlos Ernesto Carreras.

Historical Rhythms

In European literature, as in the history of European art, aesthetic disputes have oscillated between the secular antagonism which is called "the moderns" vs. "the ancients." The ancients represent the authority of classical theory; the moderns the liberty of the romantic spirit. The same question appears under different names in other aspects of culture: it is called Catholicism and free inquiry in religion, monarchy and democracy in politics, humanism and science in pedagogy. There is in European history an obvious chronological rhythm of progress and reaction: progress which tends to create new forms and reaction which tends to preserve culture within its pristine classical mold.

Greece had created archetypes, in politics, philosophy and art. The nomenclature of these disciplines is of Greek origin, as is almost all of the terminology of culture. The Romans assimilated the essence of Hellenism and spread it throughout their empire by means of the juridical system they created. The Barbarian invasion destroyed that political organization, but it was reconstructed, and one saw in the Renaissance that Greco-Latin culture still endured. From then onward, continental European civilization has been integrated and thrives on all of the continental elements. External influences precede the fall of the Roman Empire as in the case of Christianity, or they are episodic as in the case of the Arab invasion. They are transformed when they enter the existent crucible of European culture. From this point, forces from outside the continent have had less significance in Europe than those forces from its own past with their historic rhythms of tradition and revolution.

European civilization transplanted to America had within itself the impulses of classical culture. But in the new geographic atmosphere the pure species of Hellenism and Latinity became debilitated. They were of no interest to Christianity and feudalism, the forces most vigorous at the time in the Spain that colonized us. Spain, by transplanting to America an entire system of civilization, subjected the culture of our continent to predominantly extra-continental influences that have endured until today; influences increasingly vigorously pragmatic, such as industrial capitalism, and more intensely cosmopolitan, such as demographic immigration. From this results, as in every civilization of colonial origin, the anomalies of our collective development, with repercussions in literary phenomena.

We do not deny that the historical rhythms of romanticism and classicism, of monarchy and democracy, of Catholicism and free inquiry—all of which are part of European civilization—reach us also, since we are within the European cultural sphere. But it is evident that they reach us quite debilitated and that they present themselves to us sideways like the concentric waves of a geographic radiation.

Territorial ebbs of extra-continental origin have been more decisive in America than the historical rhythms inherent in the spontaneous life of a local tradition that becomes autonomous culture.

Anomalies of Our Culture

Continents are geographic organisms destined to serve as the seat of a type of culture. Once the autochthonous civilization represented by the Incas and the Aztecs had been torn apart by the European conquest, America entered into a new cultural process which is still in its beginning. American culture, when it becomes a reality, will be different from European culture.

It is already beginning to be different. In the Argentine Republic, for example, what is called the Latin question in European education has no meaning for our people; what is called the religious question is meaningless as well; and in politics the conflict of monarchy and democracy is dead. Militarism, imperialism, antisemitism are absurd words for us, although there are those who by iniquitous imitation insist in giving them, artificially, the meaning they possess in Europe. As for literary problems, the schools

referred to as classicism, romanticism, realism and decadentism degenerate here, and, like plants brought to unsuitable
climates, they become barren or they produce unexpected
fruit. Once Americans understand these phenomena, nothing will appear so ridiculous in our scholars as the eagerness
to propose to us illusory foreign models, including the imitation of the extra-continental literary styles. Each civilization is the spatial fulfillment of a culture, each culture the
temporal form of a tradition, each tradition the historical
function of the spirit of a people.

If we took a good look at the evolution of America, we
would see that the city, the origin of civilization, has always
been a fortress of military conquest or a factory of economic conquest. Our historic cities have not been born as
the result of the aggregation of rural settlers in a spontaneous cultural process, but rather by the concentration
of armed peoples coming from abroad. The American city
has not had in its genesis, therefore, the creative breath of
the native gods, as was the case with the European "polis."
For this reason our civilization is materialistic, for this reason our culture is weak. It will stop being so only when the
spirit of the land enters into the city, alien in all of its
attributes. The American spirit suffers in an atmosphere
which is not its own because historically it is European.
The European spirit also suffers in our atmosphere because
geographically it is American. The tragic nature of this
conflict is the test of colonies which became nations and
which aspire to create a culture without bedecking themselves with the trappings of a civilization mechanically transplanted to their soil.

Sarmiento saw this conflict between the Argentine city
and its pastoral hinterlands, and he summed it up in his
fortuitous antinomy: "Civilization and Barbarism." He saw
it with European eyes, and only in its political aspects during the civil war, whose consequences he suffered as an exile.
If he had seen it from an American viewpoint and with the
serenity of a philosopher, penetrating the metaphysical
essence of that phenomenon, he would have spoken other-

wise. Our cities were extra-European outposts of European culture; our hinterlands and their instinctive human forces were a new nature that struggled to make itself history, creating new aesthetic and moral forms. In my book *Blasón de Plata,* I have given another formula: "Indianism and Exoticism," which seems paradoxical to some, but which explains all the Argentine and American processes of progress and reaction, as well as the territorial character which the European historical rhythms acquire in the evolution of our culture. With it I explain the crisis of our political history and the renovations of our intellectual history.

Indianism and Exoticism

The Indians of pre-Colombian America were living in their own rudimentary culture when the European conquest that established the cities occurred. In our case, the Spaniards hispanicized the native; but the Indies and the Indians indianized the Spaniard. The *conquistadores* penetrated the aboriginal empires, destroying them; but three centuries later the peoples of America expelled the *conquistador.* The emancipation was a nativist recovery, that is to say, an indigenous recovery, against the civilizer of foreign origin. A manifesto of the Independence Movement said: "We want to expell from the country all resident Spaniards." The anthem of the Argentine Revolution sings of the event invoking the pre-Colombian Incas.

The autonomic impulse of this native revolution unfettered the smaller cities—more closely associated with American soil—against the viceroyal cities, more tied to the European tradition. It also unfettered the spirit of the hinterlands, with its Indians, its *gauchos,* and its *caudillos.* After the crisis of the civil war—which loosed the federal and democratic organization imposed by the "barbarians" of the moment—the "civilizers" opened the country to European immigration. This was necessary to the evolution of those peoples in this new period of our history. A new cycle of cosmopolitan exoticism began with this, the cycle in which we now are. Nevertheless we are already feeling the first signs of a new autochthonous creation, one which should not be martial xenophobia, but rather a peaceable creation of American culture, a nativistic recovery by way of the intellect, a spiritual conquest of our cities by the American spirit. We are moving toward this synthesis, and it will fulfill itself through a philosophic and artistic renaissance, already in view.

In the previously mentioned historical scheme we have, first, the Spanish conquerors who vanquish the pre-Colombian Indians; then the American *gauchos* who vanquish the Spanish conquerors; later, we have the European immigrants who vanquish the Argentine *gauchos:* and lastly, we shall have the autochthonous artists who will vanquish the immigrant merchants, that is to say, indianism will once again vanquish exoticism. In literary history the same pattern is repeated; first the native folklore; then the pseudoclassicism of the colonial period; then the *gaucho* poems; and later, positivism and decadentism. We are now waiting the assimilation of foreign civilization by the Indian tradition, so that its synthetic expression can appear in philosophy and art.

We see, therefore, that if the European evolution develops in chronological rhythms within its own continental tradition, then the process in America of "befores" and "afters" will be interwoven with the social tides of "here" and "there." The process involves the movement from outside to inside and from inside to outside in a type of intercontinental rhythm. This is what I have called "indianism" and "exoticism." Exoticism is necessary for our political growth; indianism is necessary for our aesthetic culture. We want neither the barbarism of the *gaucho* nor the barbarian of the cosmopolitan. We want a national culture to be the source of a national civilization, and an art that will be the expression of both phenomena.

"Eurindia" is the name of that ambition.

❧ 16 ❧

Víctor Raúl Haya de la Torre

Peruvian Reality

In 1919 Augusto B. Leguía, who had been constitu-
tional president of Peru from 1908 to 1912, seized
power. He continued to rule as a dictator for a decade.
Among other things, Leguía perpetuated the serfdom
of the Indians, supported the demands of the large
land owners, and encouraged United States invest-
ment. At the University of San Marcos, students of
Manuel González Prada (1848–1918) rejected Leguía's
programs and set forth programs of their own. The
two most important students of González Prada were
José Carlos Mariátegui (1895–1930) and Víctor Raúl
Haya de la Torre (b. 1895). In 1920 Haya de la Torre
was exiled by the Leguía government. Four years later
he announced the formation of an international party,
APRA (Alianza Popular Revolucionaria Americana)
and called for the nationalization of land and indus-
try, a united front of workers and intellectuals, the
unity of Indo-America against United States impe-

From Víctor Raúl Haya de la Torre, *Por la emancipación de
América Latina* (Buenos Aires: M. Gleizer, 1927), pp. 89–105.
Translated by the editor.

*rialism, and the internationalization of the Panama
Canal.*

*In the following letter, written in 1925 from Lon-
don to Julio R. Barcos in Buenos Aires, Haya de la
Torre discusses a number of points relevant to the
development of nationalism: the irrelevancy of the
colonial past for present-day Peru, class divisions, con-
tinentalism, and anti-North Americanism. Most important, he reviews the history of Peru and points out the
importance of the Indian to the search for national
identity.*

*Haya de la Torre's fusion of Indianism and nation-
alism has been questioned by Frank Tannenbaum in
his article "Agrarismo, Indianismo y Nacionalismo"*
(Hispanic American Historical Review, *August 1943).
Tannenbaum suggests that there is a fundamental
conflict between Indianism and nationalism. To associate the Indian with the western culture of Latin
America, he argues, one must strip him of his Indianism; therefore Indianism cannot be the basis of national identity.*

In the same way that Peru and Mexico were the centers of
Indian America, they were also centers of colonial America.
But colonial Mexico was different from colonial Peru. In
Mexico there was an attempt to create a culture. To Peru,
the Spaniards have left nothing. You have seen colonial
Lima; it is a city of adobe that subsists because it does not
rain. Mexico is a magnificent city of stone, and each one
of its great centers—Puebla, Guadalajara, San Luis, Querétaro, and so on—offers monumental remains—incomparably
superior to ours—of an era which if it was characterized by
slavery and brutal exploitation, it was also characterized by
a constructive spirit, by discipline, and by vitality. I believe
that the conquest of America was a repugnant event for us.
I believe, furthermore, that our advanced Indian empires
would have been able to perfect themselves within Western
Civilization; like Japan, they would have been able to take

advantage of it and to grow stronger while retaining their traditional systems. But it is not the time to dwell on this point. We lament the conquest, convinced that the Spaniards were ferocious in bringing it about. Nevertheless, I prefer Cortés to Pizarro, and I believe that Mexico was more fortunate with her enslavement than was Peru.

I have gone so far back in time because the Spanish conquistador, the enslaver, the oppressor, the cold egotist devoid of humanity and piety, is still in our midst. In Mexico the races have amalgamated and the new capital has been erected in the same spot where the old one used to be. The city of Mexico and the other great cities are in the heart of the country, in the mountains, in the high plains crowned by volcanoes. The tropical Mexican coast provides communication with the sea. The Mexican conquistador united with the Indian in the heartland of the mountains and forged a race which, although not properly a race in the strict sense of the word, is in fact so by the homogeneity of its customs, by the trend toward a definitive fusion of blood, and by its continuity—without violent disruption—of national life. In Peru, that did not happen. The Peruvian sierra was Indian; the real Peru remained the western Andes. The old national cities—Cuzco, Cajamarca, etc.—were banished. New Spanish cities were founded in the tropical coast where it never rains, where there are no changes of temperature, where it was possible to develop that sensual andalusian atmosphere of our happy and submissive capital.

Mountainous Peru declined. It was a field for exploitation, a place of slavery. Spanish feudalism became the order of the day, destroying a nearly perfect system of socialism. The Indian who had lived in the great community of his Empire was suddenly converted into a slave. Millions of these beings died in the mines extracting gold for their insatiable masters. The colony did not take pity on them; it insulted them, robbed them and murdered them. There was no attempt to forge any race. When it was found impossible to make the Indian of the sierra work on the coast under the implacable sun of the deep valleys, the Negro was imported. But the Indian continued to be the white man's slave, and what is unique in Peru is that that slavery continued.

Independence was for us a deceptive movement. Our real heroes of liberty were the Tupac Amarus, the Pumacahuas because they are the precursors of the liberty of the Indian. The Indian has continued before and after the political independence without any change in status. He was always the slave, the cannon fodder. He was dragged to the War of Independence, to the civil wars, and to the slaughter of the war with Chile. But the Indian, who for the most part does not speak Spanish, obeys out of terror. Ricardo Palma has said that during the war of '79 [the Indian] repeated that he was going to kill the "señor of Chile." During the Colonial period as during the time of the Republic, the Indian's desire for liberty has been the same. The Indian loves a meaningful liberty. The Indian wants the restoration of his land. For four centuries he has risen up, he has rebelled, he has let himself be killed by the hundreds, fighting in the name of hunger and of his tradition against the feudal lord who oppressed him. That is his patriotism, because that is his justice.

. . . There are no ideological or class differences among the leaders of the different ruling groups: Leguía, Pardo, Riva Agüero, Prado, Benavides, Villarán, Miró Quesada, they are all wolves of the same pack. Catholics, *gamonales* [bosses of the Indians], capitalists, bourgeois, absolutely bourgeois, there are no differences. Moreover, all have acted together, and all are united, directly or indirectly, by family and economic ties. In their various struggles, they all use more or less violent means, essentially they all represent the conservative caste, the class of the great exploiters, the neo-Spanish foreign nobility, disdainful of our reality, disposed to continue the exploitation and liquidation of the population that supports them. On fundamental questions such as the chauvinistic agitation against Chile, they are at one in their position. Each one of them struggles to be more "patriotic" than the other. The groups of intellectuals or journalists that surround each of these *caciques* also shout their hatred toward Chile, and between Leguía and the rest of them there is but one word of insult and agitation: "Chilean." Leguía calls them "Chileans" and vice-versa.

In social questions they are all reactionaries. They are all great feudal lords, or capitalists, or subjects of one or the other. The fundamental problems of the nation—those of the Indian, the land and, at the same time, that of our economic base—have never been dealt with. There has not been a single ruler who has been moved by the horror of the Indian's situation. *Gamonalismo* [bossism] is in Peru an organized and legalized crime. I have lived eight months in Cuzco, I am familiar with Cajamarca, Apurimac and other places in the Peruvian sierra. You cannot imagine the horrors that are committed there. I have seen Indians' flesh torn open by the steel bar with which they are punished. In an article published by the European and Asiatic Library of Switzerland, I made a report of what I have seen in the Peruvian sierra. The *gamonales* call the whip *hualpacaldo* (chicken soup). With it they destroy the flesh of those unfortunate beings. They kill, they rob, they burn the huts, they rape the women and the daughters with unparalleled coldness. But the *gamonal* is the deputy, the senator, the minister, the president. When I passed by Tumbes, I heard that in the coastal estate of Plateros, of which Leguía is the owner, the workers were punished by being tied up naked with their back to the sun. Tumbes is in the tropics. These tortures are well known on the coast and in the sierra of Peru.

All of this is not new. It is the kind of terror that has prevailed for a long time. The massacres of Indians and workers have taken place in Peru under all governments, since that clown Nicolás de Piérola [President, 1895–1899], who had himself cynically called "the protector of the Indian race." For this we are exiled, because we have cried out against so much horror. We have not been exiled because of the intrigues of coteries. Our generation has awak-

ened from its dream and from its patriotic stupor and from
frivolity to look clearly into the entrails of our reality. . . .
Peru is now searching for its own path. Leguía is in power,
above all, because the instinct of the people tells them to
remain with one tyrant rather than replace him with another. There are no other men on the political stage of the
dominant class. All are old, all are evil, all are hungry for
power; their vision extends no farther than their appetites.
The country is waiting for a profound change. Peru is
preparing to redeem itself definitively. To redeem itself not
only from the tyrant, but also from the class that he represents; to redeem itself from oppression and to bring about
justice for four million slaves.

For this reason it does not matter that Señor Leguía might
have told Leopoldo Lugones, his agent in Buenos Aires, that
the dissemination of our revolutionary doctrines will signify
the destruction of the Peruvian nationality and a struggle
between the races. For Leguía the nationality is the elite
who accept the horror of the present situation. This position
of Leguía is the same as that of all of the "distinguished"
men of Peru. You will see that on the day when the hour
of liberation of the people, of redemption of the Indians,
of the true and just revolution rings in Peru, the bitter
rivals of today will automatically unite. Señor Leguía, if he
is still alive, will be the common leader. "The nationality is
in danger," will be the hypocritical shout of all the groups
that make up the elite. Then there will be no more subter-
fuge; the struggle will clearly be between the miniscule
group of families that exploits the Peruvian people and that
forms the dominating class, and the people who fight for
liberty. Then the Pardos, the Aspillagas, the Prados, the
Benavides, the Riva Agüeros, and so on will form one
block; it will be the block of the bourgeois of the great
landowners, of reaction in alliance with Yankee imperialism.

Our struggle, therefore, is not only against Leguía; our
struggle is against the class that, divided or not, oppresses
the Peruvian people and sells them to the foreigner. For this
reason they have exiled those of us who have headed up or

initiated that social movement, and they have done so with the blessing of all the conservative sectors, even of those that are at the present time in temporary opposition. But although the enemy is strong, we shall always continue to advance. It is true that because of the long terror a great part of the Peruvian people is lulled, intimidated, and indifferent, but this does not mean that it does not suffer, or comprehend, or that it does not desire justice. . . .

B) 1930–1945

⚜17⚜

Getúlio Vargas

The Problem of the Iron and Steel Industry

Economic nationalism first became an important force in the development of Brazil during the rule of Getúlio Vargas (1930–1945, 1950–1954). In this 1931 speech at the Governor's Banquet in Belo Horizonte (Minas Gerais), Vargas proclaims the fundamental importance of the iron and steel industry to national development and argues for the nationalization of a number of natural resources. He does not, however, reject the use of foreign capital in the development of the country. Brazilian economic nationalism was not xenophobic during the 1930s because one of the country's major problems was to create new economic interests and not to defend existing ones.[1]

The problem that is basic to our economy is the one relating to the iron and steel industry. For Brazil, the age of

---

From Getúlio Vargas, *A nôvo política do Brasil* (Rio de Janeiro: Livraria José Olympio Editôra, 1938), I, pp. 100–103. Translated by the editor by permission of Livraria José Olympio.
[1] See John D. Wirth, *Brazilian Economic Nationalism: Trade and Steel Under Vargas* (Ph.D. Thesis, Stanford University, 1966), p. 2.

iron will mark the period of her economic prosperity. Our progress is expressed in the full utilization of this metal, the most precious of all. Development has been hindered by our lack of transportation and equipment, both indispensible for the exploitation of the material wealth with which we will overcome our immobilization.

Iron is wealth, comfort, culture, the model [of achievement] of the life of society. It makes possible the distribution of water to the cities and the irrigation of farmlands. It enables energy to be transported, industries to flourish, and factories to operate. In the land, powerful locomotives, running upon ribbons of steel, reduce distances and bring together the distant regions that exchange their products. On the waters, it is the ships, mechanically powered, that rapidly sail the seas and rivers. In the air, it is the motor of the airplane that maintains its equilibration and speeds its flight. And finally, iron goes into the beam of the ceiling, the light for the home, and, at the same time, the arms for the defense of the Patria.

I believe I can state, therefore, that the future greatness of Brazil depends mostly on the exploitation of her iron beds.

And iron is Minas Gerais.

To the people of Minas Gerais, whose very name [i.e., General Mines] in this sense indicates a certain historical predestination, falls the major effort for the conquest of this glory. Minas [Gerais] has mountains of iron with the capacity to satisfy world demand for centuries. We should exploit such resources with tenacious work and practical intelligence, thus acquiring abundance and economic independence.

We will do much in a short time if we succeed in freeing ourselves from the need to import iron goods by producing ourselves what is essential for the country. We will take a great step up the ladder toward the high destiny that awaits us by nationalizing the iron and steel industry. Our growth must come from the land, as the result of the intense development of agriculture. But the effort to achieve this growth becomes sterile and weak when we recall that all the machinery, from the plow that cuts through the earth to the truck that transports the crops, must be imported from abroad.

In order to realize this just aspiration so intimately linked to the life and to the strengthening of nationality, nearly everything depends on you, on your energy, on the vigilance of your patriotism and of your government, [an effort] worthy of the nobility of the people of Minas Gerais.

In solving this problem, in which is embodied the principal formula of our progress and upon which depends quite clearly the ascension of Brazil, you can count on the Federal Government to mobilize all available resources to aid you.

The task is arduous. Make it an ideal. The ideal is still the soul of all achievements. The same idealism that produced in the sacred mountains of Minas Gerais those brave hosts of its sons who marched to liberate the Republic, should now transform itself into a constructive idealism which will make you stoop to the rich mountain to extract from its entrails the wealth and prosperity of the Patria.

Completing, finally, my thoughts touching on the solution to this great problem, I judge it opportune to insist, again, on one point: the necessity of nationalizing the exploitation of the natural resources of the country, above all iron. I am not narrow-minded and would not commit the error of advising the repudiation of the foreign capital to be employed in the development of Brazilian industry, under the form of loans, leasing of services, provisional concessions, or many other equivalent uses.

But when it comes to the iron industry, with which we are to forge all of the equipment of our transport system and of our defense; of the improvements of waterfalls transformed into the energy which illuminates and supports the industries of peace and war; of the railroad systems of internal communication which stimulate production and in extreme cases move our armies; in this instance, I repeat, of exploitation of services of such a nature, so intimately linked to the broad and complex problem of national defense, we cannot alienate them, conceding them to foreigners. We must be farsighted and maintain the right of property and dominion over these areas.

We must realize that the Revolution, besides being a vast work of social, political and economic transformation, is also nationalist in the best sense of the word. Only superficial minds or deformed consciences do not see the profound effects of the victorious movement. No one will be able to alter this revolutionary rhythm until Brazilian aspirations are satisfied. In Brazil the Revolution started among the people with decisive aid from the Armed Forces. The Armed Forces have placed themselves at the side of the newly strengthened and invigorated Nation.

As an integral part of the patriotic multitudes that, by rebelling, have saved the nation from imminent defeat, you people of Minas Gerais, by the audacity of your deeds and the totality of your sacrifices, preeminently share the glory.

These are the words of greeting and recognition which I could not leave unsaid to the glorious people of Minas Gerais, where nature in a generous way forged within the depths of a fertile land, with the rigidity of iron, the character of its sons to whose dedication and devotion must be confided the mission of presiding over the resurgence of a new Patria.

❧18❧

Frank Tannenbaum

————◆►◆❧◆◄◆————

The Importance of
The Masters and the Slaves

In this selection, Frank Tannenbaum discusses the significance of Gilberto Freyre's books The Masters and the Slaves *and* The Mansions and the Shanties. *Freyre documents the contribution of the Negro to Brazilian society, praises Brazil's social democracy, and suggests that the mixed Portuguese and Negro race is the basis of the Brazilian nationality. Freyre's book, according to Tannenbaum, completely changed Brazil's self-image: the shame of coming from a mixed racial background was transformed into pride.*[1]

A good way to begin this introduction is to recall the many Brazilians who will tell you that in the future the history of their country will be chronicled in two parts: that before and that after Gilberto Freyre. The dividing line is

---

From Gilberto Freyre, *The Mansions and the Shanties*, translated by Harriet de Onís (New York: Alfred A. Knopf, 1963), pp. vi–xii. Reprinted by permission of Alfred A. Knopf.

[1] For further discussion of the significance of Freyre's work see *Gilberto Freyre: Sua ciência, sua filosofia, sua arte. Ensaios sôbre o autor de* Casa-Grande e Senzala, *e sua influência na moderna cultura do Brasil, comemorativos do 25° aniversário da publicação desse seu livro* (Rio de Janeiro, 1962).

Casa-Grande e Senzala (*The Masters and the Slaves*), first published in 1933, of which this volume, *The Mansions and the Shanties* (*Sobrados e Mucambos*), first published in 1936, is a continuation. The books describe the emergence and growth of Brazilian civilization from the patriarchal family, Negro slavery, and a single-crop economy—based on sugar. But *The Masters and the Slaves* is a great deal more than just a book—it marks the closing of one epoch and the beginning of another. Brazilians have in fact been carrying on what may be described as a sentimental affair with what has become for them the symbol of a new age. Since 1933, there have been eleven editions of this book in Portuguese, ten in Rio de Janeiro and one in Lisbon. While the English version of *The Mansions and the Shanties* was on press, the Brazilians published a volume celebrating the twenty-fifth anniversary of *The Masters and the Slaves*. Planned in 1958, it was four years in preparation. It is a big book—576 pages of comments, criticism, eulogy, and sheer jubilation over the first appearance of *The Masters and the Slaves*. The volume contains sixty-seven separate essays, written by eminent historians, economists, sociologists, anthropologists, novelists, poets, artists, musicians, architects, city planners, educators, doctors of medicine, geographers, linguists, diplomats, public servants, and others.

This is a tribute by the major intellectual figures of the nation to a national event—an epoch in Brazilian history. It is obvious from the subjects dealt with that Gilberto Freyre's influence has touched the nation's life at many points. There are essays about Gilberto Freyre's impact on the study of Hispanic culture in Brazil; the new literary forms in his writing; *The Masters and the Slaves* and the cultural revolution; Gilberto Freyre as seen by a Catholic; his influence on the new generation; his treatment of Brazilian culture; his work as considered by a geographer; his reinterpretation of the mestizo; Freyre as a poet; his influence on the plastic arts; Freyre as a regionalist, as a traditionalist, and as a modernist; his influence on the mural art of

Brasilia. There are interpretations of his style; studies of Freyre as an essayist; of Freyre and Brazilian cooking; of his guides to Brazilian cities; his interpretation of Brazilian reality; Freyre as a conservative and as a revolutionary; his treatment of Brazilian rural values; his impact upon Brazilian foreign policy; his influence on Brazilian literature. There are essays about the lyrical quality of his work; his new view of the Portuguese world; Freyre and the architects; his influence on the modern Brazilian novel; Brazilian philosophy in Freyre's work; Portuguese colonization in Brazil and his theory of tropicalism; Freyre as a social scientist; his influence upon history; medicine as depicted in Freyre's work; his treatment of French and English influence; Freyre and the jurists; his influence on the theater; his influence on the training of physicians; his evaluation of the Negro and the Portuguese. In these and many other areas Gilberto Freyre's work has made itself felt.

The Masters and the Slaves and *The Mansions and the Shanties* have acquired a permanent place in Brazil as national classics; other books of his are also widely known. His intellectual energy seems boundless. For, in addition to traveling, teaching, writing a regular column for Brazilian papers—an activity he began while a student—he has found time to write some twenty-five volumes and an equal number of pamphlets. Many of these have gone through more than one edition and been translated into various languages. What Gilberto's friends, followers, and admirers were celebrating, when they published a volume commemorating the first appearance of *The Masters and the Slaves,* was the work of a major creative scholar, thinker, and literary artist. In its substance and method, Gilberto Freyre's work is that of a sociologist, social historian, anthropologist, and social psychologist. He is all of these and more. He has focused a new light on the hidden recesses of the years gone by. And that light is his sense of the whole—of a culture that is infinitely complex, contradictory, riven and torn by passion, greed, generosity, love, hatred, sex, jealousy, ambition, physical voluptuousness, and the sense of art, color, music, and faith—all of this and a great deal more are part of the sum.

There is a sense of detail, of the importance of all things: the food, the cooking, the dress, the odors about the kitchen, the house, the oxen, the Negro mammy, the naked little children running about the house, the sanitation, the lighting, the window, the veranda, the master, the mistress, the governor, the emperor, the law, the lawbreaker, the judge and the criminal, the fugitive, the lash. The ways of young people with one another, the church, the priest, the friar, the school—and ten thousand other matters, all part of the record—are there, concrete and inescapable. Brazil is the unique combination of all of these things, in their tropical setting—and they are all important, equally important perhaps. The Negro slave and his master, the mistress and the colored girls about the house are equally relevant, and the vision of the author encompasses every one of them and passes judgment on none. They are bound together, and Brazil is what it is because of them, because people of many colors, races, and languages mingled, intermingled, absorbed and were absorbed, regardless of theories, views, or notions of superiority or inferiority, of better or worse, of higher or lower. One sees, through Freyre's eyes, a people emerging through time, with all of their foibles, heroism, laughter, and tears, as if through a movie camera. The mulatto mistress is carried in a sedan chair down the street by four stalwart Negro slaves, and the wife, her rival, is carried the same way down the same street at the same time. The bishop, the governor, the street urchin, and the peddler pass over the screen, playing their part in the drama and finally exchanging roles. The view is almost Augustinian, and the method infuses with life the compilation of journals, diaries, letters, photographs, newspaper advertisements, official registers, documents, books, pamphlets, songs, poems, verbal and written tradition. Synthesis, analyses, interpretation, logical deduction and induction have gone into the shaping of this work. It has all of the craft, documentation, and "jargon" that goes by the name of science in the social sciences. But in addition it has something of the Bergsonian intuition, of the poet's insight and the artist's vision. And here form becomes almost as important as substance. The literary style that carries the subject matter of *The Masters and the Slaves* and *The Mansions and the Shanties* is like a flowing stream after a storm; it is full, deep, and sparkling. It is also intimate; it has the sensitivity of sterling verse and at the same time the richness and variety of a mosaic or a tapestry, except that it is alive, changing, appetizing, and tasteful. It reminds one of Proust at his best, but it is more robust, more vivid and all-embracing. It has a wider range and a greater depth. It reveals and embraces an entire culture in formation.

The Mansions and the Shanties, the sequel to *The Masters and the Slaves,* brings the rural patriarchal society to the developing Brazilian city of the middle of the nineteenth century. The environment changes: the big house becomes the mansion, the slave quarters become the shanties, the open spaces are replaced by the city street, the spacious porch becomes the veranda, the old courtyard and its noises are replaced by the street and its sound and clatter. Instead of the familiar peddler on the plantation, there are the street crier and the vender. The splendid spatial isolation of the *Fazenda* gives way, in the mansion, to the irrepressible bombardment of the growing city, with its developing middle class, government officials, university students, books, newspapers, coffee shops, brothels, banks, society balls, and official honors. The plight of the *Fazenda* family, the patriarchate, with its polygamous traditions and authoritarian rule, is acute in this period of transition. The feudal agrarian aristocracy of the old Brazil is teased into an urban, middle-class world and converted, or half-converted, to a social democracy without completely losing its feudal paternal features.

To complete the story, one should read *Ordem e Progresso,* published in 1959, and *Região e Tradição,* published in 1941. Together these give an epic view of the growth of Brazilian culture and the Brazilian people.

Clearly, much more could be said about Gilberto Freyre's

work and its significance. What his admirers and followers have just written about him in the volume commemorating the twenty-fifth anniversary of the publication of *The Masters and the Slaves* is the start of what will, in time, be a critical review of his work at the hands of many scholars.

My own special interest in Freyre's work is not directly concerned with a critical evaluation of its substance and form. What has long seemed to me the broad significance of his work is that he has succeeded in changing Brazil's image of itself. This is a remarkable accomplishment. In only a few instances can it be said that one man, in his own lifetime, changed a great and populous nation's image of itself. The difference between the twenties and the sixties in Brazil is that today the Brazilians have discovered themselves. They have taken a good look and like what they see. They no longer wish to be Europeans, and their intellectuals no longer escape to Paris to find something to write about. They no longer describe themselves, or are so described by their own intellectuals, as a mongrel race, inferior because it consists of a mixed people. On the contrary, they find their creative freedom, their pride in the present, their confidence in the future precisely in this fact—that they are a mixed, a universal people. The social democracy of Brazil, and the pride Brazilians have discovered in being what they are, has released a font of creative enthusiasm. *The Masters and the Slaves,* published in 1933, was a revelation for the Brazilian intellectuals, artists, novelists, poets, musicians, and architects; they turned their eyes inward and began to sing a song of themselves. Hundreds of books have since been written by Brazilian scholars about Brazilian themes. They have discovered an endless task and find a ceaseless inspiration in being Brazilian and telling themselves and the world about it. This to me is the measure of Gilberto Freyre's achievement. He has given the Brazilian people a quiet pride in being what they are. As a single illustration: Jorge Amado's *Gabriela* could not have been written before *The Masters and the Slaves.*

The only other country in Latin America where a similar development has taken place is Mexico. But there it required a bloody revolution, untold suffering, and the loss of a million lives. In Brazil, it was accomplished by one man and one book.

◆§ 19 §◆

Vicente Lombardo Toledano

◆━◆▶◆◀◆━◆

The Mexican Flag
and the Proletariat

In the 1930s, Marxist labor leader Vicente Lombardo Toledano (b. 1894) attempted to preempt Mexican nationalism for the workers. He failed to do this because President Lázaro Cárdenas (1934–1940) insisted that Mexican nationalism remain a broader concept, but his arguments have had an impact on the development of popular nationalism. In his speech before the General Confederation of Mexican Workers and Farmers on February 6, 1936, included here, Lombardo Toledano responded to the charge of Monterrey businessmen that the striking workers are "Russians" and "traitors." He argues that there is no conflict between socialism and nationalism and that the workers are loyal Mexicans. In fact, he insists, the workers are the only true patriots because they are loyal to the ideas of the impoverished majority rather than those of the opulent minority.

In the clamor of the period 1910 to 1935, we again ask the

From Confederación de Trabajadores de México, *C. T. M. 1936–1941* (México: Talleres Tipográficos Modelos, n.d.), pp. 14–20. Translated by the editor.

young of today, the old of yesterday, the precursors of the
Revolution, the revolutionaries with arms, the revolutionaries with ideas, all those who have been sincere: what is the
Mexican Patria? When did it come into being? What is it?
Who formed it? How should we defend it? What should we
love in it? What should we despise in it? The question
carries us, comrades, through at least seven centuries of being placed before historical destiny; seven centuries of ask-
ing, with or without words: where is the Patria? Who is the
Patria in Mexico?

Now we have the answers. The employer class of Monterrey raises the tricolored flag and says: "This is the Patria; we
above all else, are Mexicans, and the workers of Mexico are
Russians, they are traitors to the Patria." The Patria is
Monterrey? What audacity! What cynicism! What sarcasm!
How the honorable hearts of those who have always suffered
in this Patria, those who have never even owned a pair of
sandals, rise in rebellion! (*Applause.*)

There are two Patrias in every nation of the world: the
Patria of the exploited and the Patria of the exploiters. The
Patria of the exploiters is always a smiling Patria; the Patria
of the exploited is always a Patria of tears. For this reason,
and because of the perfidious, despicable, false, cynical attitude of the employer class of Monterrey, the time has
arrived when we must recover that which is ours. We must
place these so-called patriots in the position in which they
belong, within the ranks of the traitors to the Mexican
Patria. (*Applause.*)

In Sonora, to whom does the Patria belong? A group of
landlords, a group of old and new rich; indigenous tribes,
eternal cannon fodder, shackled peasants; greedy priests in
the service of the overseer and of the new *encomendero;*
houses of prostitution in the North and miners eaten away
by tuberculosis. This is the Patria of Sonora.

In Baja California the Patria belongs to the Yankees who
own half of the land. In the South the mines also belong to
the foreigners while miners are rotted by occupational dis-

eases. These are miserable people without any possible communication with the rest of the continent. In Chihuahua, the Patria is the same; the mines belong to foreign corporations, half-naked Tarahumares scarcely speak Spanish, and Mexicans steal cattle in cahoots with American cattle thieves. There are many tombs of Villistas, many tombs of unknown soldiers who cannot rise up to declare that the Patria does not belong to Monterrey but to the hard earth of Chihuahua which furnished with the guns of many battles those who looked in anguish for something to eat. (*Applause.*)

In Coahuila, to whom does the Patria belong? Who uses it? Who holds it? Who enjoys it? Foreign corporations which own the coal region, and old and new landlords; houses of prostitution on the border, ignorance in the fields, people still without land, starvation wages. In Tamaulipas, the head of a family nominally earns a salary of one peso, but his wife, his children and his in-laws must also work to earn this sum of money. After twenty years of saving part of this miserable amount he is scarcely able to buy a pair of pants. This is the Patria of Tamaulipas. And the oil zone, whose is it? Does it belong to the pariahs of Mexico? Does it belong to the Mexican workers?

And thus, from the North to as far South as Chiapas there is shame, the common grave, the torture inflicted upon those who hold certain ideas and a certain sense of responsibility. There are droves of human beasts at the service of a German oligarchy which, with the pirates of Guatemala and of Mexico, exploits the coffee of Soconusco. There are those blinded by *onchocercosis,* those discolored by sickness that stains the skin, those tormented by enormous tumors suspended from their necks like the bells on cattle. The poor are undernourished because there are not enough *tortillas* and *chile* for them to live.

And if we go up to the region where the air is purer—to the Mexican highland so often praised by all, we see that the masses live on *pulque* because there is nothing else and because if it were not for the *pulque* they would have died of pellagra or some other disease that annihilates men when they do not have sufficient calories to survive.

This is the Patria in 1935. But the Patria of the new rich, of the millionaires, of the old rich, is not that Patria. Their Patria is brilliant, it has the press, it has schools, it has theaters, it has all that money can buy, it has all the things they wish. On the other hand, the great majority of the Mexican people—which at times has to flee to the United States in order to eat—this other Patria that they in fact form, does not have the right to stand alongside that of the millionaires of Monterrey.

For the millionaires the Patria of the poor is not the Patria, and, to defeat us, they usurp it for themselves. They unfurl the national flag and sing the national anthem in the streets and they assume the posture of men martyred by the red wave from Moscow.

They think that we loath the national flag, that we repudiate it, that we are disrespectful of it, that we do not love the Patria. What a grave error! What great ignorance! Did these poor rich people or at least their advisers not read, the Manifesto of Marx and Engels? When has socialism repudiated the Patria? When has socialism said that to destroy the Patria is a revolutionary act? Idiots! Ignoramuses! Imbeciles! Cowards! (*Applause.*)

(*The speaker unfolds a national flag.*)

This is ours, the poor, the wage earner, those who never had a Patria; it does not belong to traitors to the Mexican colors. Did they not read Juan B. Justo, the interpreter of Marx, the popularizer of Marx in South America, speaking of internationalism and Patria? And even today, ignoramuses of Monterrey, dishonest bourgeois of Monterrey, have you not heard of the recent Dimitrov trial? When those who established the fascist dictatorship in Germany accused him saying: "You do not love your country," he answered, "yes I love it, I love it because I am a socialist, because I want a country full of happy and free men, and because of this I am a patriot." (*Applause.*)

This flag does not represent corporations like those of Monterrey which enrich their managers and cheat their customers. This flag represents millions of dead Indians, rivers of blood from the War for Independence; streams of blood from the wars of the first half of the nineteenth century; more blood from the Reform; blood after Ulúa; from Valle Nacional, from all the political prisons in Mexico; blood from 1910; that of Madero, of Serdán, of the Flores Magón brothers, of the countless unknown workers and peasants who fought for the Revolution; this is blood; this is the flesh of the Mexican masses, it is not a trophy of the bandits who exploit the people. (*Applause*.)

We love the red flag, we love the red and black flag, we love all the symbols of the proletariat, because they are the sum of all the individual flags amassed with the blood of all the workers of the world. We are not traitors to the Patria; we are building a Patria, constructing a genuine Patria. The question of seven centuries must have an answer: what is the Patria? The Mexico of well-fed men who read and write and who are able to enjoy life; the Mexico, where there are no pariahs, no alcoholics, no syphilitics, only happy youth? But the bourgeoisie has not given most of the people happiness, nor has it given us hope for living. For this reason we struggle, and they think they frighten us. No! Here is our flag, here is the other, they are both our flags. (*Lombardo points to the red and black flag that covers the presidency table*.) (*Applause*.)

From this day on, starting tomorrow, let there be in every labor union headquarters the tricolored flag of Mexico together with the red flag of the proletariat. Those who have stained our country with blood, those who for centuries have sucked the blood of the defenseless masses, do not have the right to shelter themselves under this sign which is the blood of their victims! (*Applause*.)

20

David C. Jordan

Argentina's Right-Wing Nationalists

Throughout much of Latin America during the 1930s, nationalism and fascism were synonymous. This seemed logical because nationalism was often closely associated with the ideologies of right-wing elements in Argentina, Brazil, Mexico, and Peru. In the following selection, David C. Jordan, Associate Professor of Government at the University of Virginia, discusses the nature of right-wing nationalism in Argentina during the 1930s and its relationship to the Uriburu Revolution of September 6, 1930, to the program of Buenos Aires Provincial Governor Manuel Fresco and to the ideology of Juan D. Perón. Jordan points out the influence of Italy's Benito Mussolini and Spain's José Antonio Primo de Rivera on the right-wing nationalists in Argentina, their opposition to the liberalism of Sarmiento, their defense of the Catholic-Hispanic tradition, and their elite social attitudes. Perhaps most importantly, he shows how the right-

From David C. Jordan, *Argentina's Nationalist Movements and the Political Parties (1930–1963); A Study of Conflict* (Ph.D. Thesis, University of Pennsylvania, 1964), pp. 174–186. Reprinted by permission of David C. Jordan.

> *wing nationalists came to realize that to be successful*
> *they had to have popular support and link some of*
> *their ideas to those of the left-wing antiliberal na-*
> *tionalists.*

Shortly before the Uriburu coup of 1930, the right-wing antiliberal nationalists had forged an ideology. Liberal democracy had failed, social unrest was rampant—what was needed was the establishment of a strong government that would provide order and equilibrium between numbers and quality. Because of its demonstrated success, Mussolini's corporativism seemed to be the best answer. Uriburu believed in this doctrine in 1930, but his revolution failed. . . .

It is probable that . . . social attitude is the key to the right-wing nationalists, despite their heterogeneity of opinion. How a man behaves and where a man comes from is more important to them than what is accomplished. It is better that good people rule than that background and style should be sacrificed to goals. But this attitude really means that the right-wing nationalists were against class war and the domination of the Argentine nation by the culturally inferior classes. This attitude was to persist as the basic condition for granting voluntary support to Perónism later on.

Perón had been a part of the September 6 [1930] revolution. His own words on his part in that revolution demonstrated his initial sympathy with the right-wing nationalists. Perón had fascist ideas for the economy and wanted to reorganize the government. He also understood, even at this early date in his career, a democratic institutional nationalism and, consequently, that ". . . the revolution ought to have as its banner *the defense of the Constitution*. . . ." Perón took note of one other aspect of the revolution of 1930 that had future significance for his policies. This aspect was that the military revolt was poorly organized from the point of view of the percentage of military cooperation Uriburu received, and that it would have been a complete failure but for a miracle—a miracle achieved by the people of Buenos Aires. He felt that without this mass of humanity surging into the streets of Buenos Aires and shouting "Viva la revolución" the revolution might very well have failed.

Perón as well as Uriburu learned from the setbacks and successes of the September 6 revolution. They both learned that popular support was necessary for a renovating nationalist movement to be successful. . . . And it was *after* the 1930 revolution that the right-wing nationalists began to stress in earnest the economic nationalist issues that they hoped would achieve popular support while at the same time limiting participation in the government to socially acceptable people. . . .

Lugones' *La grande Argentina* came out in 1930 and attacked Anglo-Saxon imperialism, warned of the danger of foreign ownership of Argentine oil, and of the railroads. The right wing began to take many of the nationalist issues of the left-wing antiliberals, but put these issues in what they felt were the genuine traditions of Argentina.

By 1934 the right-wing nationalists had [also] become more pro-Church in their outlook. . . . In the conservative Catholic magazine *Criterio* of August 2, 1934, Gustavo J. Franceschi . . . demonstrated a conservative Catholic nationalist viewpoint. . . . Franceschi noted that he had been a member of a young group of Catholics in 1902 who had advocated a Christian democratic movement which had sought to reconstruct the social foundations of Argentine society on a corporative basis without the loss of individual liberties. . . . And in the subsequent thirty-two years he claimed that he had remained faithful to these ideas. But he suggested that to use the word "corporativismo" uncritically was not sufficient because the regimes of Salazar in Portugal, of Dollfuss in Austria, and of Mussolini in Italy were quite different. What was important was the philosophy and morality that animated the society. And Franceschi said that the regimes of Dollfuss and Salazar were to be preferred over Mussolini's because they were inspired directly from Catholic social principles. . . . Franceschi not only indicated in this social respect what were to be the right-wing aspects of Perónism, but also noted the extent to which socialist values were being incorporated into formulas acceptable to Catholic thinkers. He found, for example, value in Proudhon's socioeconomic views.

Franceschi was also anti-liberal on some economic and political issues. But he noted that it was not sufficient to be merely anti-liberal. He maintained that the anti-liberalism that had its source in the Roman Catholic Church did not exclude such sentiments as liberty, equality before the law, and the just state. . . .

Perhaps the most significant domestic event in the middle 1930's for the right-wing nationalists was the election of Manuel Fresco as governor of Buenos Aires province in 1936. His opening speech to the legislative assembly on February 18, 1936, indicated that he felt that he was continuing the fight against the Radicals begun by the Revolution of 1930. . . .

When describing Fresco's regime, that is from his election in 1936 until he was removed by [President Roberto M.] Ortiz in March of 1940, it appears to be something of a dress rehearsal for Perón's first years in power. By decree Fresco put religious education into the schools, developed cooperatives, and intimidated his opposition. Voting was turned into a public manifestation of approval. He also had an up-to-date labor code and bragged to me in an interview I had with him that during his regime there had not been one labor strike. His mentors at that time were Franco, Mussolini, and Hitler. His government was probably Argentina's first "elected" semi-fascist experiment. . . .

With so many popularizing organs [such as *Sol y Luna, El Restaurador, Ofensiva, Nueva Política,* and so on], the right wing's nationalist views were well known. The right-wing nationalists were generally Hispanists, in favor of Argentine neutrality, against the separation of the rich and the poor (in the sense they did not believe in the class war), and were, by definition, anti-Communist. They were anti-liberal as they understood the liberal value structure. From their point of view, liberalism for the economy meant *lais-*

sez faire, for politics, the sovereignty of the people, and for religion, tolerance or recognition of views other than those of Roman Catholics.

The right wing was gleeful over the coup of June 1943; especially rewarding were the initial reforms of the Army junta that included dissolution of the political parties, control of the press, and compulsory religious teaching in the schools. The right wing felt that their prayers had been answered. Marcelo Sánchez Sorondo's book *La revolución que anunciamos,* a collection of articles which had appeared in *Nueva Política,* underlined this glee.

C) 1945–present

21

Raúl Prebisch

The Economic Development
of Latin America

Since World War II, economic nationalism has in-
tensified in Latin America as many countries realized
that at least until 1960 the United States was more
interested in exchanging Latin American raw mate-
rials for U.S. manufactured goods than in helping
them develop their embryonic industry. During this
period, Raúl Prebisch, Argentine economist and for a
time Director of the United Nations Economic Com-
mission on Latin America, was one of the most im-
portant proponents of the development of industry in
Latin America. In the following selection, which is
the introductory section to a United Nations report,
he attacks the "schema" of the international division
of labor because it in fact creates disequilibrium
within the world economic system and favors the de-
veloped over the developing nations. The economic
periphery (which includes Latin America), he argues,
does not benefit by increased productivity to the same
extent as the economic center (which includes the

From Raúl Prebisch, *The Economic Development of Latin
America and Its Principal Problems* (United Nations: Department of Economic Affairs, 1950), pp. 1–7.

United States). His solution to the problem—the development of industry through export diversification and import substitution—has had considerable influence on economic nationalists throughout Latin America.[1]

In Latin America, reality is undermining the out-dated schema of the international division of labour, which achieved great importance in the nineteenth century and, as a theoretical concept, continued to exert considerable influence until very recently.

Under that schema, the specific task that fell to Latin America, as part of the periphery of the world economic system, was that of producing food and raw materials for the great industrial centres.

There was no place within it for the industrialization of the new countries. It is nevertheless being forced upon them by events. Two world wars in a single generation and a great economic crisis between them have shown the Latin-American countries their opportunities, clearly pointing the way to industrial activity.

The academic discussion, however, is far from ended. In economics, ideologies usually tend either to lag behind events or to outlive them. It is true that the reasoning on the economic advantages of the international division of labour is theoretically sound, but it is usually forgotten that it is based upon an assumption which has been conclusively proved false by facts. According to this assumption, the benefits of technical progress tend to be distributed alike over the whole community, either by the lowering of prices or the corresponding raising of incomes. The countries producing raw materials obtain their share of these benefits

---

[1] For further information on economic development and nationalism see Charles W. Anderson, *Politics and Economic Change in Latin America* (Princeton, N.J.: Van Nostrand, 1967), and Víctor L. Urquidi, *The Challenge of Development in Latin America* (New York: Praeger, 1964).

through international exchange, and therefore have no need to industrialize. If they were to do so, their lesser efficiency would result in their losing the conventional advantages of such exchange.

The flaw in this assumption is that of generalizing from the particular. If by "the community" only the great industrial countries are meant, it is indeed true that the benefits of technical progress are gradually distributed among all social groups and classes. If, however, the concept of the community is extended to include the periphery of the world economy, a serious error is implicit in the generalization. The enormous benefits that derive from increased productivity have not reached the periphery in a measure comparable to that obtained by the peoples of the great industrial countries. Hence, the outstanding differences between the standards of living of the masses of the former and the latter and the manifest descrepancies between their respective abilities to accumulate capital, since the margin of saving depends primarily on increased productivity.

Thus there exists an obvious disequilibrium, a fact which, whatever its explanation or justification, destroys the basic premise underlying the schema of the international division of labour.

Hence, the fundamental significance of the industrialization of the new countries. Industrialization is not an end in itself, but the principal means at the disposal of those countries of obtaining a share of the benefits of technical progress and of progressively raising the standard of living of the masses. . . .

The industrialization of Latin America is not incompatible with the efficient development of primary production. On the contrary, the availability of the best capital equipment and the prompt adoption of new techniques are essential if the development of industry is to fulfil the social objective of raising the standard of living. The same is true of the mechanization of agriculture. Primary products must be exported to allow for the importation of the considerable quantity of capital goods needed.

The more active Latin America's foreign trade, the greater the possibility of increasing productivity by means of intensive capital formation. The solution does not lie in growth at the expense of foreign trade, but in knowing how to extract, from continually growing foreign trade, the elements that will promote economic development.

If reasoning does not suffice to convince us of the close tie between economic development and foreign trade, a few facts relating to the situation today will make it evident. The economic activity and level of employment in the majority of the Latin-American countries are considerably higher than before the war. This high level of employment entails increased imports of consumer goods, both nondurable and durable, besides those of raw materials and capital goods, and very often exports are insufficient to provide for them.

This is evident in the case of imports and other items payable in dollars. There are already well-known cases of scarcity of that currency in certain countries, despite the fact that the amount of dollars supplied by the United States to the rest of the world in payment of its own imports was considerable. In relation to its national income, however, the import coefficient of the United States has, after a persistent decline, arrived at a very low level (not over 3 percent). It is, therefore, not surprising that, notwithstanding the high income level of the United States, the dollar resources thus made available to the Latin-American countries seem insufficient to pay for the imports needed for their intensive development.

It is true that as European economy recovers, trade with that continent can profitably be increased, but Europe will not supply Latin America with more dollars unless the United States increases its import coefficient for European goods.

This, then, is the core of the problem. It is obvious that if the above-mentioned coefficient is not raised, Latin America will be compelled to divert its purchases from the United States to those countries which provide the exchange to pay for them. Such a solution is certainly very dubious, since it often means the purchase of more expensive or unsuitable goods.

It would be deplorable to fall back on measures of that kind when a basic solution might be found. It is sometimes thought that, by reason of the enormous productive capacity of the United States, that country could not increase its import coefficient for the purpose of providing the basic solution to this world problem. Such a conclusion cannot be substantiated without a prior analysis of the factors that have caused the United States steadily to reduce its import coefficient. These factors are aggravated by unemployment, but can be overcome when it does not exist. One can understand that it is of vital importance, both to Latin America and the rest of the world, that the United States achieve its aim of maintaining a high level of employment.

It cannot be denied that the economic development of certain Latin-American countries and their rapid assimilation of modern technology, in so far as they can utilize it, depend to a very large extent upon foreign investment. The implications involved render the problem far from simple. The negative factors include the failure to meet foreign financial commitments during the great depression of the nineteen thirties, a failure which, it is generally agreed, must not be allowed to happen again. Fundamentally the problem is the same as that referred to in the preceding paragraph. The servicing of these foreign investments, unless new investments are made, must be paid for by means of exports in the same currency and, if these do not show a corresponding increase, in time the same difficulties will arise again. They will be the greater if exports fall violently. The question thus arises whether, pending that basic solution, it would not be wiser to direct investments toward such productive activities as would, through direct or indirect reduction of dollar imports, permit the regular servicing of foreign obligations.

Here one must beware of dogmatic generalizations. To assume that the meeting of foreign commitments and the proper functioning of the monetary system depend upon nothing more than a decision to obey certain rules of the game is to fall into an error involving serious consequences. Even when the gold standard was in operation in the great centres, the countries of the Latin-American periphery had great difficulty in maintaining it, and their monetary troubles frequently provoked condemnation from abroad. The more recent experiences of the large countries have brought a better understanding of some aspects of the situation. Great Britain, between the two wars, encountered difficulties somewhat similar to those which arose and continue to arise in the Latin-American countries, which have never taken kindly to the rigidity of the gold standard. That experience doubtless helps to bring about a better understanding of the phenomena of the periphery.

The gold standard has ceased to function, as in the past, and the management of currency has become even more complex in the periphery. Can all these complications be overcome by a strict application of sound rules of monetary behaviour? Sound rules for these countries are still in the making. Here there arises another vital problem; that of utilizing individual and collective experience to find a means of harmoniously fitting monetary action into a policy of regular and intensive economic development.

Let this not be interpreted as meaning that the classic teachings are of no value. If they do not provide positive rules, they at least show what cannot be done without impairing the stability of the currency. The extremes to which inflation has gone in Latin America show that monetary policy was not based upon these teachings, since some of the larger Latin-American countries increased circulation to a greater extent than did those countries which had to meet enormous war expenditure.

These facts must be taken into account in an objective analysis of the effects of the inflationary increase on the process of capitalization. It must, however, be admitted that, in most of the Latin-American countries, voluntary savings are not sufficient to cover the most urgent capital needs. In any case, monetary expansion does not bring about an increase in the foreign exchange reserves necessary for the importation of capital goods; it merely redistributes income. It must now be determined whether it has led to a more active capital formation.

The point is a decisive one. The raising of the standard of living of the masses ultimately depends on the existence of a considerable amount of capital per man employed in industry, transport and primary production, and on the ability to use it well.

Consequently, the Latin-American countries need to accumulate an enormous amount of capital. Several have already shown their capacity to save to the extent of being able to finance a large part of their industrial investments through their own efforts. Even in this case, which is exceptional, capital formation has to overcome a strong tendency towards certain types of consumption which are often incompatible with intensive capitalization.

Nevertheless, it does not appear essential to restrict the individual consumption of the bulk of the population, which, on the whole, is too low, in order to accumulate the capital required for industrialization and for the technical improvement of agriculture. An immediate increase in productivity per man could be brought about by well-directed foreign investments added to present savings. Once this initial improvement has been accomplished, a considerable part of the increased production can be devoted to capital formation rather than to inopportune consumption.

How are sufficient increases in productivity to be achieved? The experience of recent years is instructive. With some exceptions, the rise in employment necessitated by industrial development was made possible by the use of men whom technical progress had displaced from primary production and other occupations, especially certain comparatively poorly paid types of personal services, and by the employment of women. The industrial employment of the unemployed, or ill-employed, has thus meant a considerable improvement in productivity and, consequently, where other factors have not brought about a general lowering of productive efficiency, a net increase in national income.

The great scope for technical progress in the field of primary production, even in those countries where it has already been considerable, together with the perfecting of existing industries, could contribute, to national income, a net increase that would provide an ever-increasing margin of saving.

All this, however, especially in so far as it is desired to reduce the need for foreign investments, presupposes a far greater initial capitalization than is usually possible with the type of consumption of certain sectors of the community, or the high proportion of national income absorbed, in some countries, by fiscal expenditure, which makes no direct or indirect contribution to national productivity.

It is, in fact, a demonstration of the latent conflict existing in these countries between the desire to assimilate, quickly, ways of life which the technically more advanced countries adopted step by step as their productivity increased, and the need for capitalization without which this increase in productivity could not be achieved.

For the very reason that capital is scarce, and the need for it great, its use should be subjected to a strict standard of efficacy which has not been easy to maintain, especially where industries have developed to meet an emergency. There is, however, still time to correct certain deviations and, above all, to avoid them in the future.

In order to achieve this, the purpose of industrialization must be clearly defined. If industrialization is considered to be the means of attaining an autarchic ideal in which economic considerations are of secondary importance, any industry that can produce substitutes for imports is justifiable. If, however, the aim is to increase the measurable well-being of the masses, the limits beyond which more intensive industrialization might mean a decrease in productivity must be borne in mind.

Formerly, before the great depression, development in the Latin-American countries was stimulated from abroad by the constant increase of exports. There is no reason to suppose, at least at present, that this will again occur to the same extent, except under very exceptional circumstances. These countries no longer have an alternative between vigorous growth along those lines and internal expansion through industrialization. Industrialization has become the most important means of expansion.

This does not mean, however, that primary exports must be sacrificed to further industrial development. Exports not only provide the foreign exchange with which to buy the imports necessary for economic development, but their value usually includes a high proportion of land rent, which does not involve any collective cost. If productivity in agriculture can be increased by technical progress and if, at the same time, real wages can be raised by industrialization and adequate social legislation, the disequilibrium between incomes at the centres and the periphery can gradually be corrected without detriment to that essential economic activity.

This is one of the limits of industrialization which must be carefully considered in plans of development. Another concerns the optimum size of industrial enterprises. It is generally found in Latin-American countries that the same industries are being attempted on both sides of the same frontier. This tends to diminish productive efficiency and so militates against fulfilling the social task to be accomplished. The defect is a serious one, which the nineteenth century was able to attenuate considerably. When Great Britain proved, with facts, the advantages of industry, other countries followed suit. Industrial development, however, spurred by active competition, tended towards certain characteristic types of specialization which encouraged profitable trade between the various countries. Specialization furthered technical progress and the latter made possible higher incomes. Here, unlike the case of industrial countries by comparison with those producing primary products, the classic advantages of the division of labour between countries that are equal, or nearly so, followed.

The possibility of losing a considerable proportion of the

benefits of technical progress through an excessive division of markets thus constitutes another factor limiting the industrial expansion of these countries. Far from being unsurmountable, however, it is a factor which could be removed with mutual benefit by a wise policy of economic interdependence.

Anti-cyclical policies must be included in any programmes of economic development if there is to be an attempt, from a social point of view, to raise real income. The spread of the cyclical fluctuations of the large centres to the Latin-American periphery means a considerable loss of income to these countries. If this could be avoided, it would simplify the problem of capital formation. Attempts have been made to evolve an anti-cyclical policy, but it must be admitted that, as yet, but little light has been thrown on this subject. Furthermore, the present dwindling of metallic reserves of several countries means that, in the event of a recession originating abroad, they would not only be without a plan of defense but would lack means of their own to carry out the measures demanded by the circumstances.

❧22❧

Richard W. Patch

———◆◆◆———

Peasantry and National Revolution: Bolivia

Richard W. Patch, Professor of Anthropology at the State University of New York at Buffalo, has written extensively on Bolivia and the Revolution of 1952. In this essay, he makes the important point that the nationalism that developed out of the Bolivian Revolution was internally cohesive and directed toward the goals of planning and integration. The semifeudalism of prerevolutionary Bolivia was incompatible with the nation, Patch argues, but the Revolution has begun to involve the Indian in the national community and has thus created a genuine basis for the construction of the nation.

Nationalism as well as revolution had been vindicated. The turn which nationalism took may be the most significant point which the Bolivian case lends to our understanding of nationalism.

The new nationalism had nothing to do with reaction against colonialism or imperialism. It was a response to

From Kalman H. Silvert (ed.), *Expectant Peoples: Nationalism and Development* (New York: Vintage Books, 1967), pp. 109–115. Reprinted by permission of Alfred A. Knopf.

Western ideals of government, a consequence of technological aspirations which require a high degree of integration, a
result of new ideas of justice which destroyed the existing
class structure. This nationalism was internal, directed towards domestic goals of planning and integration, not a
nationalism directed at the rest of the world. Its intellectual
explanation drew on ideas which had grown slowly since
1920, suffered reverses, and had not yet combined into a
system sufficient to account for the sweeping change.

The first formal step was seizure of the tin mines. The
government decree, however, affected only the largest holdings, properties of two nationals and an Argentine who
were popularly believed to have controlled previous governments. Smaller holdings were not affected, and even a large
U.S. firm, W. R. Grace and Company, continues operations.
The government-controlled mines did not become an economic success for many reasons, but their removal from private hands in 1952 was a political necessity. Tin is the country's symbol of national wealth. To proceed with the level-
ing of special interest groups would have been impossible
while the three major owners received an income larger than
the national budget.

Another part of the revolution was the dismemberment of
the already discredited army. The methods exceeded democratic bounds—officers and men were imprisoned until they
were proved subservient to the MNR, or they were politically neutralized and relegated to menial civilian employment. The army was replaced as an effective force and national symbol by civilian militia and armed tin miners and
farmers. The transfer of the means of power to the latter
solidified the interdependence of the MNR leaders and the
masses, and made certain the eventual absorption of the
miners and Indians into national society.

A third reform brought the miners and Indians into one
more dimension of national life: a new electoral law enfran-
chised all citizens without regard to their literacy. The literacy requirement had previously limited the vote to the
urban upper classes and the rural landowners. The rest of

the population, mostly Aymará and Quechua speakers, had no written language and thus were doubly barred from the polls. Given the existing system of education there was little likelihood of their learning Spanish or writing in any language. The reform gave them the vote and, considering their numbers, the ultimate control of elections.

An educational reform gave promise of bringing Spanish and literacy to the younger Indians over a period of years. But the rapid pace of events leading to national integration and a self-conscious Bolivia of all Bolivians was not to await the amalgamation which education might bring in a generation.

Other basic changes centered, as might be expected, around a program of agrarian reform. Tempting as it may be to read into the reform the vision of a government determined to distribute land and meeting with a large measure of practical success in breaking up feudal estates and giving the Indians control over the countryside, it would be a mistake to overemphasize the government's intent or to minimize the role which the Indians themselves played in organizing and in precipitating the reform. In fact, the government part in reform consisted of providing the machinery for the resolution of disputes and the formalization of land redistribution. But it was the unexpected organization of the Indians, their warfare on the landowners, and their own expropriation of land which furnished the driving force of the reform. The formalities should not be mistaken for the fundamental motor force.

It was Indian participation in the Chaco War which made possible the rapid growth of an autonomous Indian organization. During the war the Quechua speakers in particular were impressed by their sudden introduction to the idea of "Bolivia," the notions of citizenship and fatherland, and the inflammatory concept of their equality with Spanish speakers. If they were equal in their obligations to the nation, how could their privileges be less? The war was lost, the army disbanded, but the Indians who returned to the serfdom of semi-feudal estates did not forget their new ideas.

Indians, mainly veterans, formed groups for the purpose of renting land for cash payments to escape the onerous obligations of the *latifundia* system in which they were given usufruct of small plots in exchange for three to six days of unpaid labor each week for a *patrón*. These organizations were suppressed by the landowners, but the suppression increased the cohesion of the Indians, who for the first time felt persecuted as a group rather than exploited as individuals. The organizations, called "agrarian syndicates," turned to school construction and other group activities when their attempts to rent land were frustrated. The syndicates grew slowly, but came under firm Indian leadership in the 1940s. They took no direct part in the 1952 revolution, but with the breakdown of army and police authority in the provinces after April 1952 the organizations spread widely and rapidly among the Quechua speakers, mainly in the heavily Indian department of Cochabamba. The Aymarás were never recruited with the same success. Finally the syndicates were strong enough to challenge the landowners, many of whom resisted the full implications of the revolution for several months in 1952. When the challenge broke into open battle, the major landowners were driven into the cities or into exile. The Indians carried out their own land distribution, even taking houses, vehicles, and machinery. The government was still preoccupied with the army and the nationalization of the mines, but the threat of civil war between rural and urban populations precipitated quick action to establish a formal agrarian reform council and requisite procedures. Studies were made and a decree drafted and ceremonially signed by the president and his full cabinet at a gathering of some 500,000 Indians in the remote Indian village of Ucureña on August 2, 1953. The "Indians"—actually so mixed that the racial appellation no longer applied—dropped the designation of *indio* and insisted they were *campesinos,* or "rural folk." Social change was outstripping economic change.

The foundation of national integration, the prerequisite of valid nationalism, had been laid. Full accomplishment of the task would await not only political stability and a work-able economy, but also countless social and ideological adaptions to the new class structure and to the acculturating peasants.

The accomplishment of full integration is doubly difficult now because the drastic reforms undertaken in so short a time have seriously unbalanced the economy and upset long-standing political institutions. In this predicament the government can take nothing for granted but must attempt many different approaches at once, some in conflict with others. The results so far are not spectacular. The non-dramatic social advancement of the peasants is overshadowed in many minds by the crumbling economy and the destruction of the former elite. But many persons misunderstand the exclusiveness of alternatives in true revolution. The impressive fact is that the Bolivian government, in its state of perpetual crisis, has turned neither to communism nor to attacks on other nations as ways of distracting attention from the problems of moving in ten years from insularity to responsible and conscious nationhood.

Bolivian nationalism is an extraordinary thing. It is not the work of a man or group of men, or of a party. The success of the MNR in promoting nationalism came about not because it had originated the idea but because it seized on the themes of nationalism and revolution which had been imbedded in the public mind ever since they provided the rationale for reaction against the constitutional order of the few in 1920 and for the Chaco War. The internally directed nationalism of the 1950s corresponded closely to the long latent pressure of the Indians to become mestizos, and their potential for acculturation to the modes of the Spanish-speaking society. The MNR in giving voice and direction to strong currents of ideas became in part the creature of changes it had initiated itself. The study of nationalism becomes the study of the interplay of forces; of governed and governors, goals and economic realities, peasants and wage-earners—not the study of policy, intent, or party leaders.

Nationalism as Social Integration in the Emergent Nation

As we have seen, not all nationalism is reaction against empire. On the contrary, the nationalism we are examining is the product of the decay and collapse of internal institutions which supported merely a loosely affiliated state that focused on the political individual rather than structure, on the geographical community rather than the nation, on the social elite rather than the mass. Clearly this nationalism is not the same as the outwardly oriented nationalism of states recently freed from imposed dominion whose institutions, from social classes to political bureaucracy, remain virtually untouched in the transition from colony to nation.

Bolivian nationalism is representative of the new nationalism of underdeveloped countries which have long enjoyed statehood, but statehood that existed only for an elite which maintained its domination of the masses through feudal obligations and the maintenance of allegiances on a community level. The subjection of the great majority of the population *depended* on the nonexistence of the nation; the power of the elite *depended* on nonadaptation to the new forces tending toward democracy and mobility which modern technology, war, and mass communications made irresistible. The result was inability on the part of the elite either to control or to conform to the seemingly inevitable procession of collapse, revolution, democracy of a sort, nationhood, and a nationalism inwardly oriented toward rebuilding the shattered society, economy, and polity. Similar situations led to the Civil War in Spain and to the Russian revolution. It is an ominous truth that the Bolivian revolution of 1952 was only the second such breakdown and struggling reformation in Latin America.

Institutional breakdown and social reintegration. The most striking feature of the Bolivian case is the breakdown of the *latifundia* and the cultural accommodations or acculturation of the former Indian peons (*colonos, pegujaleros,* and the many other terms in use) to the encompassing mestizo culture. Bolivia is an especially interesting example of mass emergence because 60 per cent of its population are speakers of Indian languages—Quechua and Aymará. It is true that not all of these persons lived as serfs on the large *latifundia*—a few were small landowners, some lived in theoretically communal communities, some were sharecroppers on small mestizo holdings. But the greater number were serfs on the large estates which date far back into colonial times and which formed the world for most of their residents. The obligations of the peon were truly feudal. He was assigned a small plot of land which he held at the pleasure of the landowner. In return he gave the landowner from three days of work each week (in the Cochabamba valley) to six days (on parts of the high plateau) with no recompense except a ration of coca. If the lands of the *patrón* did not suffice fully to occupy this supply of labor, the peon could be rented to another landowner or even sent out to domestic service for the profit of the lord. If the peon were for any reason unable to serve he had to provide a substitute. In addition the peon owed a certain period of service each year for such special offices as caring for the horses and mules (*mulero*); keeping the door of the estate house at night (*portero*), or feeding the fires of the great chimneys which open on the outside of the house and warm a brick shell extending into the sleeping quarters.

The wife of the peon was required to give a similar period of service (*pongüeaje*) in the house of the *patrón,* as cook, maid, maize sheller, *chuño* maker, or whatever other work was in season or desired. When the date was fixed for the marriage of a peon's daughter, she was required to spend a period, usually a month, in residence at the house of the parish priest. This practice was theoretically to receive religious instruction, but actually it was the priest's way of securing domestic service, and not infrequently of exercising a *droit du seigneur*. Children spent most of their time caring for the cattle and sheep of the landowner, taking them to the high and often dangerous pastures. If any livestock was lost the peon was responsible for its replacement. In addition to this immense levy of labor, the lord made levies in kind: spun wool, maize beer, and the like. And finally he exacted a cash tribute, the ancient *canon*. The system and even some of its nomenclature date back far beyond the time of the Spanish conquest. Parts of it were familiar to Charlemagne.

Most urban Bolivians were ignorant of the functioning of this system, thinking of it, if at all, as a benign paternalism in which the estate owner generously cared for the sick, stood godfather (*padrino*) for christenings, and gave money to bury the dead. They did not realize that nearly all landowners lived not on their estates but in the large cities or at best in neighboring mestizo towns. The estate house was visited only at long intervals, often in the spirit of a vacation. The day-to-day operations were left to a hired administrator whose proximity to *cholo* status bred a contempt and a brutality toward the Indians comprehensible to those in the United States who are familiar with the relations in the South between poor whites and Negroes. These institutions have disappeared in Bolivia and many would have us believe that they never existed. The doubter has only to visit the high sierra of Peru to see it still in full operation, and then to talk to a resident of Lima who will tell him that the abuses of the *latifundia* were legislated out of existence years ago.

A country atomized by *latifundia* is hardly a breeding ground for nationalism. It is in fact the opposite. A nationalistic state cannot maintain feudalism; a feudalistic state cannot support nationalism without destroying its own foundations. The latter is what happened in Bolivia. The immediate result need not be nationalism; it can be totalitarianism and a straining social reorganization bordering on chaos, as was the case for a generation in Mexico. Nationalism has emerged, somewhat tentatively, in Bolivia because the imported and manufactured ideas of the elite are paralleled by a remarkable integration of the formerly Indian population into an emergent national society and a true base for a nation-state.

◦§23§◦

Gustavo Rojas Pinilla

———◆▸◆◂◆———

The Armed Forces and
the Colombian Patria

*On June 13, 1953, Lt. Gen. Gustavo Rojas Pinilla
led the Colombian Armed Forces in the overthrow of
President Laureano Gómez. Rojas Pinilla acted with
the support of the Liberals and the moderate Conservatives to avoid civil war. The next day he made
the following brief speech to the people of Colombia
in which he justified the action of the Armed Forces
on the basis of their special trust to defend the Patria.*

*This speech, and the Armed Forces' assumption of
the role of guardian of the nation, is not atypical of
military nationalism in Latin America. The same
ideas were expressed by the Brazilian Humberto
Alencar Castelo Branco when he overthrew the regime
of João Goulart in April 1964, and by the Argentine
Juan Carlos Onganía when he overthrew the regime of
Arturo Illia in June 1966.*

Colombians:

In light of the country's tremendous political crisis, the
threat to public order, the national restlessness, and other

From *El Tiempo* (Bogotá, June 15, 1953), p. 11. Translated by
the editor.

events with important moral implications which culminated in the untimely and unconstitutional dismissal of President Urdaneta Arbeláez, the Minister of War, and high officers of the military, the Armed Forces of the Republic have decided to take charge of the government. The Armed Forces have acted thus because they are loyal to the supreme trust which historically has been bequeathed to them by the Liberator, Simón Bolívar, and by the Patria itself. The Armed Forces are motivated solely by the spirit which for a long time has guided all good Colombians along the paths toward unity. The Armed Forces will lead Colombia along the paths of order which will produce authentic justice for all, true progress without discrimination of any kind for all the local communities, and an ennobling peace. All of this is in harmony with the teachings of Christ our Lord, and of the Liberator Simón Bolívar. The Armed Forces appeal to all Colombians of good will who are not corrupted by base party passions, personal motives, private interests, and family concerns to join a crusade to support the traditional authority of the Patria, putting it above the interests of castes or groups.

No more blood, no more depredations in the name of any political party, no more quarrels among the sons of the same immortal Colombia! Peace, law, liberty, and justice without discrimination for all. This is particularly important for the classes less favored by fortune, for the proletariat and the indigent. The Patria will not rest while some of its sons are hungry and without clothing. The Armed Forces will remain in power while they create the conditions in which we can hold free elections. These elections, under a genuinely democratic system, will produce the chief executives, the legislators, and the leaders which the Colombian people want.

Through the person of their supreme commander, the Armed Forces have made every possible effort to find means other than those which they have been obliged to adopt in order to safeguard the nation.

Faithful to the traditions of this Republic, the government will maintain its international obligations and will live up to every commitment previously made. I send a heartfelt greeting to the valiant Colombian forces which are fighting at the side of the United Nations in Korea.

In behalf of the Armed Forces—trustees of the sacred heritage of the Liberator—which have gained control of the entire national territory without spilling blood, let me urge you to work for a just and strong Colombia.

◄§ 24 §►

Alfonso Ferrari Amores

October 17

On October 17, 1945, the descamisados, the "shirtless" followers of Juan D. Perón in Argentina, rose up and demanded the release of their imprisoned leader. The Armed Forces of the country decided to turn over their prisoner rather than risk a civil war, and Perón went on to become president for nearly a decade. The following selection written by an obscure Argentine, Alfonso Ferrari Amores, is not good poetry, but apparently it was effective propaganda. Amores carefully associates Perón and his wife Evita with the redemption of the nation, the Argentine hero of independence José de San Martín, and with the common people in their struggle against the oligarchy. He expresses well the popular nationalism which Perón carefully cultivated.

Before that date, during our lives,
the decadent oligarchy, the moribund epic.

From Antonio Monti (ed.), *Antología poética de la revolución justicialista* (Buenos Aires: Librería Perlado, 1954), pp. 55–56. Translated by the editor.

There were the statues and the swords,
and the epic hymns, the trustworthy proof.
Oh Patria! Images! Frozen seeds!
The ancient glory absent, no new glory.

Your blood sucked, like Croesus the vampires
were contemplating. Oh Martyr! Your formerly heroic vein
now dry. They rejoiced in it. The children of your pain
sunken in lethargies of mummies and papyrus.

No longer austere Spain, but the Nordic Midas,
enervated your strength, deaf to the clarion;
and in vain inflamed Nemesis called for
the second crusade of our San Martín.

In vain! The sluggish fat of the Sepoy
was sleeping in the shadow of another's flag,
and from the red fringes [of the flag] hanging down to the
      tunic [of the Sepoy oligarchy]
a baptism of the zebra of a neutral chameleon.

That could have been Gomorrah and Sodom,
the abject ending, could not be ours.
God kept vigil, and he wanted to raise us like Lazarus
above the coma with a firm and skillful hand.

This hand had a name. Your name, Juan Perón!
And, potent, it overflowed the boundaries without limits,
the people, the people clamors for redemption.
Arms become columns, heads become battering rams.

Re-creator of the Patria, free of caudillismo,
a name also held your sacred inspiration.
Our tenth Muse, that of Justicialism:
Your name, Eva Perón!

The gaze of the oligarchs recognizes us again;
their eyes of bronze become moist when they contemplate us.

So much time without seeing us!
So much without embracing us!
Oh restored Patria! Your cry covers the earth:
October 17! October 17!

25

Hêlio Jaguaribe de Mattos

A Succinct Analysis of
Brazilian Nationalism

In Brazil in recent years, much attention has been devoted to the relationship between economic nationalism and development. Some, such as the young writer of the Catholic left Cándido Antônio Mendes de Almeida, argue that the only way to free Brazil (and the rest of the third world) from its semicolonial status is to pursue a policy of national development which rejects all outside help.[1] Others, such as Hêlio Jaguaribe de Mattos, the founder of the Instituto Superior de Estudos Brasileiros, argue that the goal of nationalism is independence, social justice, and national harmony brought about by economic development under the leadership of the national bourgeoisie. He insists that nationalism is effective only if it furthers development and, unlike Cándido Mendes, he is willing to accept outside help if it contributes to this

---

From Hêlio Jaguaribe, *Burguesía y proletariado en el nacionalismo brasileño* (Buenos Aires: Ediciones Coyoacán, 1961), pp. 20–25. Translated by the editor.
[1] See Cándido Antônio Mendes de Almeida, *Nacionalismo e Desenvolvimento* (Rio de Janeiro, Instituto Brasileiro de Estudos Afro-Asiáticos, 1963).

goal. *In the following selection, Jaguaribe provides a brief description of Brazilian nationalism with particular emphasis on its economic aspects.*

From the Historical to the Political Nation

In the historical sense the formative process of the Brazilian nation began with the colonization. But in the political sense only during the recent decades of the twentieth century were the conditions created which would force a national configuration upon Brazil.

Since the colonial beginnings, Brazil was guided into an economic system which complimented that of Europe, a system in which the country specialized in the exploitation of raw materials and primary products for external consumption. Slavery was the system by which this economic function was carried out and Brazil remained subject to slavery until the end of the past century. Thus, until recently, Brazil lacked the conditions and the stimuli for better integration. Such conditions, had they been in effect, might have turned the country inward toward itself and created a new focus for action.

The political movements which led to Independence and the Republic were superficial in that they scarcely altered the colonial or semicolonial economic institutions. Of much greater importance were the socioeconomic transformations which, from the abolition of slavery, began to create an internal market. As a result of the demands of the growing internal market and of limited imports, the country began to industrialize.

Development and Nationalism

Within the limits of this study there is no room for an analysis of these transformations. It should be noted, however, that the development of the Brazilian economy, initiated during the years of the First World War, continued with the crisis of 1929 and intensified after the Second World War. This development forced the country to turn inward, to produce for internal consumption, to adapt its social structure to the nature and the situation of its own classes, to think about its own problems, and to model its institutions under the pressure of its own social forces. This internal transformation—which dates back to 1920 and the Revolution of 1930, but which was most noticeable from the 1940s on—was not effected in a uniform and homogeneous way. At the same time that different sectors of Brazilian life were experiencing this transformation, the demand for the integration of the country as a whole was making itself felt. Such a demand, as we already observed, originates when in the historical sense it manifests itself in a community objectively characterized as a nation, for the political purpose of definitively and fully shaping the nationality. This is the purpose of nationalism.

In the Brazilian case, as was indicated, nationalist movements came forth fragmentarily and discontinuously, reflecting socioeconomic development. There was a cultural nationalism in which the modernist movement and the currents which began within it were related. More recently, economic nationalism burst forth to regain possession of national capital in the form of state monopolies and the exploitation of oil and atomic minerals. And at the same time political nationalism developed. It was identified internally with the demands of democracy and social justice, with the tendency to strengthen the Union within the structure of a federation, and with the revitalization of the municipality as a basic regional center. In foreign relations, political nationalism demands greater autonomy from the United States and the great European powers, and inclines us toward a neutralist line in the conflict between the United States and the Soviet Union. It expresses the consciousness of Brazil's own interests with regard to other nations, the rights of the masses within the country, and respect for popular sovereignty and all that is national.

The Sociology of Nationalism

The economic development of Brazil has influenced the sociological aspects of nationalism. In the semicolonialism of pre-1930 Brazil, the ruling classes were governed by the logic of our dependence on outside elements. The Brazilian people were subjected by a law of near slavery to the soil, and were destined to produce the articles with which they competed for the loans of the North Americans and the Europeans. The logic of our economy imposed upon the ruling classes a vision of the world centered on those foreigners who provided so many of their consumer goods. The working masses had no means of defending their interests in this productive system in which prices were fixed externally by the buyer market.

The transformations brought about by economic development changed that system. Parallel to the sectors of the ruling classes that remained tied to the economy of exploitation of primary goods, there came forth and acquired increasing importance sectors dedicated to production for the internal market. This small but growing dependence on national consumption provided the working masses with the means to demand a more just redistribution of the national income.

The controversy between nationalism and cosmopolitanism is essentially the debate between the social structures tied to the old productive regime and those of the new. The traditional forces aspire to maintain the relative importance that they had in the Empire and in the Old Republic. They favor liberal economic policies to the degree to which free trade strengthens the primary sector of the economy, but they argue, according to the position defined by Celso Furtado, that the country is responsible for the fluctuations of foreign prices. With regard to the primary sector of the economy, they want the "privatization" of profits and the "socialization" of losses. On the other hand, the new forces tied to development favor industrialization by means of protectionism and the redistribution of wealth. They seek to direct the internal order of the country and they demand the full affirmation of its sovereignty.

The cosmopolites underestimate the national capacity for accumulation of capital and for the incorporation of modern technology within the system, and therefore believe that national progress depends on foreign investment. They favor a neocolonialist policy especially with regard to the United States; they believe the role of the United States is to expand the Brazilian economy by investing its capital and technology as it did in Canada. The nationalists overestimate the national capacity for investment and especially the technical preparation of the country. They are suspicious of foreign investment and they favor a policy of state capitalism, attributing to the public powers the principle obligation to promote the economic development of the country.

The debates surrounding oil and atomic minerals, the management of foreign capital, and more recently tariff reform, manifest these two positions. The controversy surrounding the new tariff law is typical. The forces tied to the primary economy asked for the complete abolition of state controls on commercial exchanges with the exterior, seeking to regain control of a single exchange market in which the rates would be determined freely by supply and demand. The forces tied to industrialization saw in the tariff a new protectionist mechanism and they opposed any exchange reform which might abolish state control and the differentiation of rates. The Union of the Iron and Steel Industry published a statement in which it expressed the point of view that only through a transfer of wealth from the primary sector to basic investments, made possible by the multiplicity of rates, would it be possible to promote Brazilian economic development.

Psychology of Nationalism

If we examine the subject from a psychocultural point of view, we see that the nationalist and cosmopolitan positions correspond to well-defined levels of mentality and culture. Those groups which include the most basic and the most sophisticated levels of mentality and culture acknowledge the predominantly nationalist tendency, while the middle level groups are more emphatically cosmopolites.

Nationalism is an aspiration associated on the one hand with the more dynamic sectors of the bourgeoisie engaged in the industrial revolution. On the other hand it is associated with the proletariat whose capacity to consume increases with industrialization. Also, the technicians, administrators, and intelligencia of the middle class, tied simultaneously to the process of development and to the internal and external consolidation of the state, are of the nationalist tendency. Cosmopolitanism is the position of the land-owning-commercial bourgeoisie—the leadership sector of the bourgeoisie in the semicolonial and underdeveloped conditions of the Empire and the Old Republic—and of a large part of the middle class.

The definition of opinions by levels of mentality and culture is also related to issues of both nationalism and cosmopolitanism. The simple affirmation of confidence in the potentialities of the country, unconscious of national limitations, leads the most rudimentary and uncivilized mentalities to an unconditional xenophobic nationalism. On the other hand, a consciousness of the limitations of the country and the frustration caused by them, aggravated by comparisons with the fully developed countries, generates an inferiority complex that sterilizes the national sentiment and tends toward cosmopolitan ideals. Only where there is a clearly defined and superior cultural base does one find the successful critic of the critic and the negation of the negation. Thus, to have a critical conscience but to be deprived of a system of reference leads the Brazilian to despise his own country and inspires in him a cosmopolitanism of compensation. Comprehension, sociologically and historically qualified by Brazilian reality, leads to the conviction that the country can transform and develop itself at a very favorable rate, and that it will in a short time transform itself into a great nation, sustaining for itself a national orientation.

26

Jânio Quadros

Brazil's New Foreign Policy

Many of the leaders of the countries of Asia, Africa, and Latin America have attempted to maintain their independence of thought and action in the Cold War era by pursuing a neutral foreign policy. One of these people, Jânio Quadros—president of Brazil from January 31 to August 25, 1961—upset the United States by supporting Fidel Castro, by favoring debate on China's admission to the United Nations, and by seeking to establish relations with Russia and the Eastern European countries. In the following article Quadros clearly states his reasons for following this course. Foreign policy, he insists, must be an instrument of national development. In order that Brazilian foreign policy be such, the country must strengthen its ties to the developing world, particularly Africa, and must firmly oppose colonialism without denying its Western tradition. Brazil must maintain diplomatic and trade relations with all countries and must remain neutral in the Cold War.

From *Foreign Affairs Quarterly*, vol. 40, no. 1 (October 1961), pp. 19–27. Reprinted by permission of *Foreign Affairs*. Copyright © 1961 by the Council on Foreign Relations, Inc., New York.

The interest shown in the position of Brazil in international affairs is in itself proof of the presence of a new force on the world stage. Obviously my country did not appear by magic, nor is it giving itself momentarily to a more or less felicitous exhibition of publicity seeking. When I refer to a "new force," I am not alluding to a military one, but to the fact that a nation, heretofore almost unknown, is prepared to bring to bear on the play of world pressures the economic and human potential it represents, and the knowledge reaped from experience that we have a right to believe is of positive value. . . .

Because of our historical, cultural and Christian background as well as our geographical situation, ours is a predominantly Western nation. Our national effort is directed toward the achievement of a democratic way of life, both politically and socially. It may not be idle to stress here that our dedication to democracy is greater than that of other nations of our same cultural sphere. We have thus become the most successful example of racial coexistence and integration known to history.

Common ideals of life and organization draw us close to the major nations of the Western bloc, and on many issues Brazil can, in a leading position, associate itself with this bloc. This affinity is underlined by our participation in the Inter-American regional system, which entails specific political commitments.

However, at the present juncture, we cannot accept a set national position exclusively on the basis of the above premises. It is undeniable that we have other points in common with Latin America in particular, and with the recently emancipated peoples of Asia and Africa, which cannot be ignored since they lie at the root of the readjustment of our policy, and on them converge many of the main lines of the development of Brazilian civilization. If it be true that we cannot relegate our devotion to democracy to a secondary place, it is no less true that we cannot repudiate ties and contacts offering great possibilities for national realization.

The closeness of Brazil's relations with neighboring countries of the continent and with the Afro-Asian nations, though based on different reasons, tends to the selfsame end. Among these, in the majority of cases, are historical, geographic and cultural motives. Common to them all is the fact that our economic situation coincides with the duty of forming a single front in the battle against underdevelopment and all forms of oppression.

From all this, naturally, certain points stand out that may be deemed basic to the foreign policy of my government. One of these is the recognition of the legitimacy of the struggle for economic and political freedom. Development is an aim common to Brazil and to the nations with which we endeavor to have closer relations, and the rejection of colonialism is the inevitable and imperative corollary of that aim.

It is, furthermore, in the light of these political determinants that today we consider the future of the Inter-American regional system of first importance. The growth of Latin America as a whole and the safeguarding of the sovereignty of each nation of the hemisphere are the touchstones of a continental policy as the Brazilian government understands it. . . .

The United States must realize that today it confronts a challenge from the socialist world. The Western world must show and prove that it is not only Communist planning that promotes the prosperity of national economies. Democratic planning must also do so, with the assistance of those economically able, if the political system of a perplexed two-thirds of the Western world is to avoid the risk of bankruptcy.

We cannot too often stress the extent to which poverty separates us from North America and the leading European countries of the Western world. If by their success these represent, in the eyes of underdeveloped peoples, the ideal of achievement of the élite of European cultural origin, there nevertheless is taking root in the minds of the masses the conviction that this ideal, for a country without resources and hamstrung in its aspirations for progress is a

mockery. What solidarity can there be between a prosperous nation and a wretched people? What common ideals
can, in the course of time, withstand the comparison between the rich, cultivated areas of the United States and
the famine-ridden zones of the Brazilian Northeast?

Thinking of this sort irrevocably creates in us a sense of
solidarity with those poverty-stricken peoples who, on three
continents, are struggling against imperialist interests which,
under the umbrella of democratic institutions, mislead—if
not destroy—attempts to organize popular economies. When
nations competing with the democratic group make demon-
strations of real or pretended and disinterested economic
help, this problem seems more acute under the pressure of
the conflict of interests.

At this point it might be appropriate to refer to the ideological prejudices of the capitalist democracies, ever ready
to decry the idea of state intervention in countries where
either the state controls and governs economic growth—
which has become a question of sovereignty—or nothing at
all is achieved. We are not in a position to allow the free
play of economic forces in our territory, simply because
those forces, controlled from outside, play their own game
and not that of our country.

The Brazilian Government is not prejudiced against foreign capital—far from it. We stand in dire need of its help.
The sole condition is that the gradual nationalization of
profits be accepted, for otherwise it no longer is an element
of progress but becomes a mere leech feeding on our national effort. Let it be known that the state in Brazil will not
relinquish those controls that will benefit our economy by
channeling and ensuring the efficiency of our progress.

Economic imbalance is doubtless the most critical of all
the adverse factors that beset the Inter-American regional
system, and from it almost all others stem. My government
is convinced that it is fighting for the recovery of Pan
Americanism and that this must start with the economic
and social fields. Politically we are trying to give shape and

content to the imperative principles of self-determination and non-intervention, and it is these principles that guide us in relation to the Americas as well as to the rest of the world.

The still dramatically present question of Cuba convinced us, once and for all, of the nature of the continental crisis. In defending with intransigence the sovereignty of Cuba against interpretations of an historical fact which cannot be controlled *a posteriori*, we believe we are helping to awaken the continent to a true awareness of its responsibilities. We stand by our position on Cuba, with all its implications. Surely the Brazilian attitude has been understood by other governments, and as it gains ground, the entire regional system shows signs of a regeneration in the assessment of the responsibilities of each member nation.

The government of the United States, through its recent aid programs, took an important step toward the revision of its classical and inoperative continental policy. We hope that President Kennedy, who is not lacking in the qualities of leadership, will carry the revision of his country's attitude to the very limit and will sweep away the considerable remaining obstacles on the road to a truly democratic, continental community.

As to Africa, we may say that today it represents a new dimension in Brazilian policy. We are linked to that continent by our ethnic and cultural roots and share in its desire to forge for itself an independent position in the world of today. The nations of Latin America that became politically independent in the course of the nineteenth century found the process of economic development delayed by historical circumstances, and Africa, which has only recently become politically free, joins us at this moment in the common struggle for freedom and well-being.

I believe that it is precisely in Africa that Brazil can render the best service to the concepts of Western life and political methods. Our country should become the link, the bridge, between Africa and the West, since we are so intimately bound to both peoples. In so far as we can give the nations of the Black continent an example of complete absence of racial prejudice, together with successful proof of progress without undermining the principles of freedom, we shall be decisively contributing to the effective integration of an entire continent in a system to which we are attached by our philosophy and historic tradition.

The attraction exerted by the Communist world, by Communist techniques and by the spirit of Communist organizations upon the countries but recently freed from the capitalist yoke is common knowledge. Generally speaking, all underdeveloped countries, including those of Latin America, are susceptible to that appeal. It must not be forgotten that whereas the independence of the Latin American nations was inspired by a liberation movement rooted in the French Revolution, the autonomy obtained by the new Asian and African nations was preceded by a wave of hope aroused by the socialist revolution in Russia among the oppressed classes and peoples all over the world. The Afro-Asian liberation movement arose against the domination by nations that compose—if not lead—the Western bloc.

These historical factors are of decisive importance and must be borne in mind when gauging the role that a country such as Brazil can play in the task of reappraising the dynamic forces that are at work in the new world of today in Asia and Africa.

For many years Brazil made the mistake of supporting European colonialism in the United Nations. This attitude —which is only now fading—gave rise to a justified mistrust of Brazilian policy. Misinformed circles, overly impressed with European patterns of behavior, contributed to a mistake which must be attributed more to a disregard of the deeper commitments of our country than to political malice. Our fraternal relationship with Portugal played its part in the complacency shown by the Ministry of Foreign Affairs of Brazil in this matter.

Therefore, everything points to a necessary change of position with regard to colonialism, which in all its guises

—even the most tenuous—will from now on meet with the determined opposition of Brazil. This is our policy, not merely in the interests of Africa, nor for the sake of a platonic solidarity, but because it is in keeping with Brazilian national interests. These to a certain extent are still influenced by the most disguised forms of colonialist pressure, but call for a rapprochement with Africa.

I might add that the raising of the economic standards of the African peoples is of vital importance to the economy of Brazil. Even from a purely selfish standpoint, we are interested in seeing the social betterment and improvement in the production techniques of Africa. The exploitation of Africans by European capital is detrimental to the Brazilian economy, permitting as it does the fostering of commercial competition on the basis of low-salaried Negro workers. Competition on a civilized and human level must be found to replace that of enslavement by underpayment of an entire race. Here and now, the industrial growth of my country guarantees to the Africans a most important source of supply, which could even serve as the basis for arrangements for the linking together of our respective production systems. . . .

Here I must underscore another important aspect of the new Brazilian foreign policy. My country has few international obligations: we are bound only by pacts and treaties of continental assistance which commit us to solidarity with any member of the hemisphere that may become the victim of extra-continental aggression. We have not subscribed to treaties of the nature of NATO, and are in no way forced formally to intervene in the cold war between East and West. We are therefore in a position to follow our national inclination to act energetically in the cause of peace and the relaxation of international tension.

Not being members of any bloc, not even of the Neutralist bloc, we preserve our absolute freedom to make our own decisions in specific cases and in the light of peaceful suggestions at one with our nature and history. A group of nations, notably of Asia, is also careful to remain on the sidelines in any clash of interests which are invariably those of the great powers and not necessarily those of our country, let alone of world peace.

The first step in making full use of the possibilities of our position in the world consists in maintaining normal relations with all nations. . . .

The world must be made aware of the fact that Brazil is intensively increasing its production, looking not only to the domestic market, but specifically seeking to attract other nations. Economically speaking, my government's motto is "Produce everything, for everything produced is marketable." We shall go out to conquer these markets: at home, in Latin America, in Africa, in Asia, in Oceania, in countries under democracy, and in those that have joined the Communist system. Material interests know no doctrine and Brazil is undergoing a period where its very survival as a nation occupying one of the most extensive and privileged areas of the globe depends on the solution of its economic problems. Our very faithfulness to the democratic way of life is at stake in this struggle for development. A nation such as ours, with 70,000,000 inhabitants and with the world's highest rate of population growth, will not permit even a slowing down of its movement toward the full utilization of its own wealth.

Without fear of error I can say that the experiment in democratic progress being carried out in Brazil is decisive both for Latin America and for all the underdeveloped areas of the world. Therefore, this experiment is of deep interest to prosperous nations which are also proud of being free. They will remain so to the extent that success crowns the efforts for economic emancipation of the underdeveloped nations living under the same system. Freedom once again becomes the outgrowth of equality.

It must be pointed out that the idea behind the foreign policy of Brazil, and its implementation, has now become the instrument for a national development policy. As part and parcel of our national life, foreign policy has ceased to be an unrealistic academic exercise carried out by oblivious and spellbound élites; it has become the main topic of daily concern. With it we seek specific aims: at home, prosperity and well-being; elsewhere, to live together amicably and in world peace.

27

Richard R. Fagen

━━━◆●◆━━━

Enemies, Friends, and Cuban Nationalism

On New Year's Day in 1959, Fidel Castro came to power in Cuba and initiated a new phase in that country's history. Practically from the beginning the United States and Cuba were at odds with each other and this conflict has had an important influence on Cuban nationalism. In the following selection, Professor Richard R. Fagen makes a scholarly analysis of the relationship between nationalism, internationalism, and the Cuban world view. For examples of the radical left-wing nationalism of which Professor Fagen speaks, the student should read Castro's Second Declaration of Havana and some of the works of former Guatemalan president, Juan José Arevalo.[1]

In order to understand the appeal and the content of the current Cuban world view, it is necessary to appreciate its

From David J. Finlay, Ole R. Holsti, and Richard R. Fagen, *Enemies in Politics* (Chicago: Rand McNally, 1967), pp. 217–225. Reprinted by permission of Rand McNally.

[1] *Revolución* (Havana), V, 573 (February 5, 1962); *The Shark and the Sardines* (New York: Lyle Stuart, 1961) and *Anti-Communism in Latin America* (New York: Lyle Stuart, 1963).

historical antecedents and its development. Since at least the time of José Martí and the Spanish-American War, antagonism toward the United States has been a recurring theme in Cuban politics, although its earlier volume and pervasiveness never approached the level attained under Castro after 1960. The most fully institutionalized pre-Castro expression of anti-Americanism came in the first years of the Party of the Cuban Revolution or *Auténticos* which was founded in the 1930's. The 1935 program of the *Auténticos* was organized around the symbolic triumvirate of "nationalism, socialism and anti-imperialism." By nationalism was meant national independence and development, and by anti-imperialism was meant disengagement from North American political and economic control. But long before the *Auténticos* began to broadcast their own particular brand of anti-Americanism, publicly expressed dislike for the "Colossus of the North" was heard on the island. For example, in 1922, after developments in the sugar trade and the sugar industry considered by many Cubans to be inimical to their interests, one Havana newspaper printed the following two-page headline: "Hatred of North Americans Will Be the Religion of Cubans." "The day will have to arrive," the paper continued, "when we will consider it the most sacred duty of our life to walk along the street and eliminate the first American we encounter." Fidel Castro has seldom used more virulent language.

The tapestry of anti-Americanism from Martí through the *Auténticos* to Castro is not, however, all of one piece. Much of the rhetoric and symbolism—the bloated Uncle Sam, his pockets stuffed with dollars and guns, the Wall Street millionaires hand in hand with corrupt Latin American politicians and landowners—are common to most varieties of Cuban nationalism. Similarly, the themes of North American economic exploitation, political domination, and the necessity for Latin solidarity in the face of Yankee aggression continue at least sporadically throughout the twentieth century. But the specific sins attributed to the

Yankees have changed through time, as changing political
and economic relations in the hemisphere have offered first
one and then another "target of opportunity" to the nationalists. Furthermore, the involvement of Cuba with the
Soviet Union and Eastern Europe has added an entirely new
dimension to the tapestry. Cuban anti-Americanism before
1960 was not thrown into relief by positive references to
any other country or any other form of social organization.
Except for a pantheon of idealized Cuban and Latin American heroes, the rhetoric introduced no abstract good guys,
only bad. At that time, Cuban nationalism looked to indigenous sources for a definition of the right, the proper,
and the civilized, whereas it looked north of the Rio Grande
for a definition of the evil, the immoral, and the barbaric.
After Castro, however, and particularly after the Bay of
Pigs, positive models for the construction of the new Cuba
were sought not only in the Cuban past, real and imagined,
but also in Soviet theory and practice. While anti-Americanism continued unabated, Cuban nationalism became ad-
mixed with internationalism, albeit internationalism of a
very special type.

The revolutionary elite draws on the history of Cuba in
a most selective manner. The pivotal and most positive
historical figure is, of course, José Martí who since 1959 has
been credited, at one time or another, with foreshadowing
by word or by deed almost every tenet of the revolutionary
creed. Symbolic homage is also paid to the heroes of the
Ten Years' War (1868–1878) and particularly to the three
leading generals of the War of 1895 against Spain. The
revolutionary leaders, however, find little to praise in the
history of Cuban politics after 1900. There are a few exceptions, the most notable being Julio Antonio Mella, student
leader and first Secretary-General of the Communist Party
of Cuba. Mella is now canonized as the archetypical young,
revolutionary martyr. But in general, the parade of indigenous nationalists after the Spanish-American war is ignored
in Cuba today; those leaders are dismissed by the revolu-

tionaries as having been hopelessly bourgeois, compromised, and corrupt.

If the regime can find few domestic heroes from 1900 to the advent of Castro, it does not, however, lack for devils. The catalogue is impressive: the dictators Machado and Batista, Presidents Grau and Prío, the North American marines, the Platt Amendment, the sugar interests, and Yankee businessmen, gangsters, and politicians, to mention only the most important. Only with the advent of Castro to national prominence in 1953—the date of his abortive attack on the Moncada Army Barracks—does the negativism of the revolutionary view of the recent past begin to be counterbalanced by positive elements. Now a new generation of revolutionary heroes appears, doing battle against dictatorship at home and against imperialism both on the island and abroad. Castro and his lieutenants stand at the head of the new gallery of heroes, but the ranks are filled with hundreds of lesser-known Cubans, mostly young and mostly dead. . . .

Thus, the Castro regime has drawn selectively on Cuban history for both gods and devils to inform its current mobilization efforts. To these historical symbols, as we have seen, have been added others which evoke no such echoes from the past. There are new actors on the stage: the Soviet Union, Eastern Europe, the Afro-Asian bloc, and a host of Cuban heroes created by the revolution itself; all are evaluated in overwhelmingly positive terms. Nevertheless, the negative elements of the total Cuban world view continue to outweigh the positive elements; enemies are still quantitatively and qualitatively more important than friends. Why should this be so? Is the hemispheric political environment in which the revolution moves really as hostile as the leaders claim? If not, why do they continue to organize public communication around the dominant theme of inevitable antagonism between the United States and Cuba?

It is extremely difficult to separate the real from the imagined Cuban grievances against the United States. Speaking of the pre-Castro period, apologists for the Cuban side are ready and able to cite chapter and verse to substantiate their claim that for 60 years the United States controlled the politics, plundered the resources, humiliated the population, and crippled the economy of the island. Defenders of United States policy are just as quick to list manifold social and economic benefits that accrued to the Cubans because of the American presence. Yet for our purposes we need attempt no detailed reconciliation of these two extreme interpretations of the historical record, for consistent with both are three key assertions. First, the degree of American political involvement in Cuba was considerable. For example, the Platt Amendment, in which "Cuba consents that the United States may exercise the right to intervene for the preservation of Cuban independence, the maintenance of a government adequate for the protection of life, property and individual liberty," was in effect from 1901 to 1934. Second, the degree of American economic involvement in Cuba was even greater. A U.S. Department of Commerce survey published in 1956 stated that in Cuba "the only foreign investments of importance are those of the United States. American participation exceeds 90 percent of telephone and electric services, about 50 percent in public service railways, and roughly 40 percent in raw sugar production. The Cuban branches of United States banks are entrusted with almost one-fourth of all bank deposits." Third, without arguing for either the morality or the immorality of this political and economic involvement, without taking sides with either those who claim that the American presence stunted Cuban development or those who claim that it accelerated the economy, we can agree that it must have been extremely galling to Cuban nationalists to live for 60 years in the political and economic shadow of the United States. . . .

Turning to the Castro period, there was a rapid disintegration of Cuban-American relations and a concomitant rise of anti-Americanism during 1959, the regime's first year in power. By January of 1961, when the U.S. broke diplomatic relations with Cuba, the revolutionary image of the United States was already being presented in the negative and strident language reflected in the poetry and the editorials. Once again, to explain the course of events leading to this antagonism, apologists for both sides point accusing fingers at the other. Referring to 1959 and 1960, the Cubans cite American aid to Batista, opposition to the first agrarian reform and later nationalization laws, attacks by Miami-based exiles, termination of military and technical aid, refusal to refine Soviet crude oil, reduction of the U.S. quota for Cuban sugar, economic embargo on U.S. goods shipped to Cuba, and espionage and subversion by U.S. agents. The American spokesmen can muster an equally long list of Cuban provocations and misdeeds: illegal executions, Communist infiltration in government, expropriation without compensation, destruction of press autonomy, recognition of Communist China, increasing economic dependence on the Soviet bloc, export of revolution to the hemisphere, and unjustified attacks on U.S. officials, citizens, policies, and property. Again, however, for our purposes we need not attempt a reconciliation of these two points of view. Whichever side was "right" and whichever "wrong," it is clear that an interactive and self-supporting system of threat and counterthreat, misunderstanding and countermisunderstanding, and retaliation and counter-retaliation was established between Cuba and the United States in 1959 and 1960. By 1961, the antagonism had congealed, and further moves by both sides, the Bay of Pigs invasion, the embrace of Marxism-Leninism, the missile crisis, U.S. over-flights and Cuban hemispheric mischief-making, only served to reinforce existing hostility.

The current Cuban world view, and particularly the image of the United States, thus draws support from four sources. First, traditional Cuban nationalism provides a language and a set of symbols which give the anti-Americanism of the revolution historical roots and legitimacy. Second, the revolutionary movement itself has generated a new capital fund of nationalistic symbols on which the leaders

can draw to dignify the movement and deprecate its enemies. Third, U.S.-Cuban relations before 1959 left a legacy
of mutual misunderstanding and real grievances which have
been exploited by the Castro government to explain and
sustain current antagonisms. Fourth, U.S.-Cuban relations
after 1959 gave rise to a fresh series of real grievances used
by the leadership to structure and intensify hostility.

As emphasized earlier, by calling events such as the Platt
Amendment, U.S. ownership of public utilities, the reduction of the sugar quota, and the Bay of Pigs invasion real
grievances, we do not mean to imply that the Cubans were
wholly innocent in any instance of triggering the relevant
historical sequence. What is meant is that large majorities
of politically aware Cubans perceived and continue to
perceive these and other events as attacks on the political
sovereignty, economic autonomy, and territorial integrity
of the island. The Castro government did not have to
invent the Bay of Pigs invasion and the economic blockade;
they are real and unambiguously hostile acts no matter what
their historical genesis and justification. There is, therefore,
a ring of truth about Cuban charges against the United
States, a credibility which the charges of other radical nationalists often lack. The official and publicly repeated
policy of the American government *is* the destruction of
the Castro regime, now by economic strangulation and
diplomatic isolation, and earlier by support of armed invasion. When most other radical leaders claim that the im-
perialists are trying to do away with them, their charges
are not so fully authenticated by the hostile words and acts
of a great power.

The Cuban world view, however, is not completely explained by references to Cuban nationalism and Cuban-
American relations, past or present. As India, Algeria, and
many other cases suggest, there is no law of politics which
dictates that indigenous nationalism and a history of stormy
relations lead a nation inexorably toward inflexible hostility
to the old dominant power and a deep dependency on a
new. The factors outlined so far suggest that the Cuban

world view is sufficiently rooted in history and reality to satisfy minimum requirements of political credibility, but the same factors do not explain why the leaders attach so much importance to its content, promulgation, and maintenance. In order to understand these phenomena, we must look at the revolution itself and at the men who made it.

One of the most striking features of the revolution is how enmeshed it has been in international politics since Castro first took power. Many of the most salient events in the life history of the revolution have involved directly one or more foreign powers. The expropriation of lands and businesses, the flight of the refugees, the Bay of Pigs, the missile crisis, the exportation of revolution, and economic dependency on the Communist bloc are some familiar examples. This level of international involvement, but not its precise content, is a consequence of the radicalism of the revolutionary elite and the opportunities generated by the East-West conflict. Almost immediately, and with marked impatience, the revolutionary elite set out to transform Cuban society, destroying the old order and building the new. Because the United States was so deeply involved in the old order, a clash of some magnitude was inevitable, for the transformation envisaged by the leaders could not be made except at the expense of the Yankees. Furthermore, building the new order at breakneck speed placed demands on the Cuban economy and polity which could not be met with domestic resources, either material or ideological. By means of Leninist politics and Soviet economic aid, the elite sought to continue and even accelerate the radical transformation of a society which possessed neither the indigenous capital nor the manpower to transform itself in accordance with the revolutionary blueprint. Thus, within two years after the overthrow of Batista, Cuba was deeply entangled in Cold War politics, perhaps to a greater degree than any other small nation in the world.

The internationalism of the revolution is reflected in the mobilization efforts of the leadership. We noticed earlier that almost two-thirds of the *El Mundo* editorials were focused on the international environment, and this ratio of external to internal attention is also found elsewhere in Cuban public communication. The revolution fails and succeeds, lives and dies, by what happens in the rest of the world. Domestic politics is inextricably linked to international politics. It is thus not surprising that the elite expends so much time and energy in an attempt to structure and evaluate for the masses the world political stage on which the drama of the revolution is being played. Both symbolically and actually, the revolution only makes sense when viewed in its international context. Moreover, as the poetry illustrates, the elite has blurred by word and action the conventional line separating the domestic and the foreign. The two environments have been mixed, and from the mixture a new ordering of the political landscape has emerged. In the new symbolism, geography does not count. Rather, the dimension of support-nonsupport for the revolution is paramount. Those who give aid and comfort to the regime are friends; all others are enemies. "Foreign" means antagonistic to the leadership and its actions; and the language of nationalism is made elastic enough to warm with praise new friends who live half-way around the world.

Still, however, we have not come to grips with the important functional questions. Why, as Castro says, does the revolution need enemies? Or conversely, in addition to the necessity of military protection and economic aid, why does it need friends? Put more generally, in what manner is the revolutionary map of the political environment related to the dynamics of the Cuban system? History, nationalism, and the surge of radicalism have provided the symbols and the opportunities exploited in programs of public communication; but these factors do not by themselves fully explain the passion, the jealousy, and the thoroughness with which the leadership guards and promulgates the new world view.

This new world view is intended to serve the regime in the following four ways: (1) by establishing the identity and the meaning of the revolution; (2) by legitimizing the revolutionary leaders and their programs; (3) by providing a spur to action and a rationale for participation; and (4) by defining new models of development and new modes of behavior. Success in all of these tasks is considered crucial to the continuation of the revolutionary system. From this derives the priority given to the diffusion, maintenance, and public acceptance of the officially sanctioned images of enemies and friends.

Bibliographical Notes

Although the literature on nationalism and related subjects is extensive, not much of it is particularly useful. For the most part this material is excessively descriptive, polemical, or conceptual in the most abstract and unuseable manner. This bibliography is highly selective, but it includes the works I have found most useful and many of them include bibliographies of additional material. I have limited the references primarily to works in English although I have listed some of the most essential books in Spanish and Portuguese. In addition, I have concentrated on general works pertaining to nationalism in Latin America and to those dealing with Argentina, Brazil, and Mexico.

The best studies of the general historical development of nationalism are Carlton J. H. Hayes, *The Historical Evolution of Modern Nationalism* (New York, 1931); Friedrich O. Hertz, *Nationality in History and Politics* (London, 1944); Hans Kohn, *The Idea of Nationalism* (New York, 1960); and Royal Institute of International Affairs, *Nationalism* (London, 1939). Some of the more informative general studies about recent nationalism are E. H. Carr, *Nationalism and After* (London, 1945); Karl W. Deutsch, *Nationalism and Social Communication* (New York, 1953); Rupert Emerson, *From Empire to Nation* (Boston, 1962); Harvard University Center for International Affairs, *United States Foreign Policy: Ideology and Foreign Affairs* (Washington, 1960); Carlton J. H. Hayes, *Nationalism: a Religion* (New York, 1960); Barbara Ward Jackson, *Nationalism and Ideology* (New York, 1966); and Louis L. Snyder, *The New Nationalism* (Ithaca, N.Y., 1968). Perhaps the two most important collections of essays on nationalism are Karl W.

Deutsch and William J. Foltz (eds.), *Nation-Building* (New York, 1966) and K. H. Silvert (ed.), *Expectant Peoples* (New York, 1967). Harry G. Johnson (ed.), *Economic Nationalism in Old and New States* (Chicago, 1967) is excellent and the editor's essay in which he sets up a theoretical model of economic nationalism, is particularly useful. Louis L. Snyder (ed.), *The Dynamics of Nationalism* (Princeton, N.J., 1964) is also well done. For additional bibliography see Boyd C. Shafer, *Nationalism: Interpreters and Interpretations,* Publication No. 20 of the Service Center for Teachers of History of the American Historical Association (Washington, 1959); Koppel S. Pinson, *A Bibliographical Introduction to Nationalism* (New York, 1935); and Karl W. Deutsch, *An Interdisciplinary Bibliography on Nationalism, 1935–1953* (Cambridge, Mass., 1953).

There is no definitive study of nationalism in Latin America, but the student might well begin with the pioneering study of Arthur P. Whitaker, *Nationalism in Latin America: Past and Present* (Gainesville, 1962) and with Arthur P. Whitaker and David C. Jordan, *Nationalism in Contemporary Latin America* (New York, 1966). Other works of significance are Victor Alba, *Nationalists without Nations* (New York, 1968); Robert J. Alexander, "Nationalism, Latin America's Predominant Ideology," *Journal of International Affairs* (Fall, 1961); Daniel Cosío Villegas, "Nationalism and Development," in Mildred Adams (ed.), *Latin America: Evolution or Explosion?* (New York, 1963); Robert N. Burr (ed.), "Latin America's Nationalist Revolutions," *The Annals of the American Academy of Political and Social Science* (March 1961); Charles C. Griffin, "An Essay on Regionalism and Nationalism in Latin American Historiography," *Journal of World History* (1962); John J. Johnson, "The New Latin American Nationalism," *Yale Review* (December 1964); Gerhard Masur, *Nationalism in Latin America* (New York, 1966); Robert E. Scott, "Nation Building in Latin America," in Deutsch and Foltz, *op. cit.;* and Irving L. Horwitz, Josué de Castro, and John Gerassi (eds.), *Latin American Radicalism, A Documentary Report on Left and Nationalist Movements* (New York, 1969).

Samuel L. Baily, *Labor, Nationalism and Politics in Argentina* (New Brunswick, N.J., 1967) provides a good introduction to nationalism in Argentina and includes an extensive bibliography. Other published works on Argentina are Noberto Ceresole, *Ejército y política nacionalista* (Buenos Aires, 1968); Earl T. Glauert, "Ricardo Rojas and the Emergence of Argentine Cultural Nationalism," *Hispanic American Historical Review* (February 1963); Marysa N. Gerassi, *Los nacionalistas* (Buenos Aires, 1968); Juan José Hernández Arregui, *La formación de la conciencia nacional (1930–1960)* (Buenos Aires, 1960); John J. Kennedy, *Catholicism, Nationalism, and Democracy in Argentina* (Notre Dame, Ind., 1958); Alberto Methol Ferré, *La izquierda nacional en la Argentina* (Buenos Aires, 1963); and K. H. Silvert, "The Costs of Anti-Nationalism," in Silvert, *op. cit.* The following Ph.D. dissertations contain important information on the subject: Marvin Goldwert, *The Argentine Revolution of 1930: the Rise of Modern Militarism and Ultra-Nationalism in Argentina* (University of Texas, 1961); David C. Jordan, *Argentina's Nationalist Movements and the Political Parties (1930–1963): A Study of Conflict* (University of Pennsylvania, 1964); James R. Levy, *The Development and Use of the Heroic Image of José de San Martín: 1840–1900* (University of Pennsylvania, 1964); and Winthrop R. Wright, *Argentine Nationalism and the Growth of Railways* (University of Pennsylvania, 1964).

E. Bradford Burns, *Nationalism in Brazil: a Historical Survey* (New York, 1968) focuses primarily on cultural nationalism but contains a good bibliographical essay. In addition the student should consult Frank Bonilla, "A Nationalist Ideology for Development: Brazil," in Silvert, *op. cit.;* José Honório Rodrigues, *The Brazilians: Their Character and Aspirations* (Austin, Tex., 1967); Hélio Jaguaribe, *O nacionalismo na atualidade brasileira* (Rio de Janeiro, 1958) and the same author's "The Dynamic of Brazilian Nationalism," in Claudio Véliz (ed.), *Obstacles to Change in Latin America* (New York, 1965); Barbosa Lima Sobrinho, *Desde quando somos nacionalistas?* (Rio de Janeiro, 1963); Hermínio Martins, "Ideology and Development: 'Developmental Nationalism' in Brazil," in Paul Halmos (ed.), *Latin American Sociological Studies* (The Sociological Review Monograph No. 11, 1967); Nelson Werneck Sodré, *Raízes históricas do nacionalismo brasileiro* (Rio de Janeiro, 1960); Cândido Mendes de Almeida, *Brazilian Nationalism and Development* (New York, 1968); and John D. Wirth, *Brazilian Economic Nationalism: Trade and Steel Under Vargas* (Ph.D. Thesis, Stanford University, 1966).

Considering the fact that most scholars agree that Mexico is perhaps the only genuine nation in Latin America, it is surprising that more books are not specifically devoted to the topic. Frederick C. Turner, *The Dynamic of Mexican Nationalism* (Chapel Hill, N.C., 1968) is the most wide ranging and has a good bibliography. Other works of importance are John S. Brushwood, *Mexico in Its Novel: A Nation's Search for Identity* (Austin, Tex., 1966); Peter G. Earle, "La nacionalidad mexicana," *Cuadernos Americanos* (November–December 1964); Floyd F. Ewing, *Carranza's Foreign Relations: An Experiment in Nationalism* (Ph.D. Thesis, University of Texas, 1952); Manuel Gamio, *Forjando patria* (Mexico, 1960); Peggy A. Korn, *The Beginnings of Mexican Nationalism: The Growth of an Ideology* (Ph.D. Thesis, University of Pennsylvania, 1966); Albert L. Michaels, *Mexican Politics and Nationalism from Calles to Cárdenas* (Ph.D. Thesis, University of Pennsylvania, 1966); *Mural Painting of the Mexican Revolution: 1921–1960* (Mexico, 1960); Andrés Molina Enríquez, *Los grandes problemas nacionales* (Mexico, 1909); and Edward H. Worthen, *The Reconquest of Mexico: A Panoramic View of Mexican Literary Nationalism* (Ph.D. Thesis, University of Michigan, 1965).

There are many works on nationalism in Latin American countries or areas other than Argentina, Brazil, or Mexico. Among the most important are Richard N. Adams, "Nationalization," in *Handbook of Middle American Indians,* VI (Austin, Tex., 1967); Jesús Chavarría, *José Carlos Mariátegui, Revolutionary Nationalist: the Origins and Crisis of Modern Peruvian Nationalism, 1870–1930* (Ph.D. Thesis, University of California at Los Angeles, 1967); Charles E. Frazier, Jr., *The Dawn of Nationalism and Its Consequences in Nicaragua* (Ph.D. Thesis, University of Texas, 1958); Ernest Halperin, *Nationalism and Communism in Chile* (Cambridge, Mass., 1965); C. A. M. Hennessy, "The Roots of Cuban Nationalism," *International Affairs* (London, July 1963); Philip J. Houseman, *Chilean Nationalism, 1920–1952* (Ph.D. Thesis, Stanford University, 1961); and Sybil Lewis and Thomas G. Mathews (eds.), *Caribbean Integration* (Rio Piedras, P.R., 1967).

BORZOI BOOKS ON LATIN AMERICA

Under the General Editorship of Lewis Hanke,
UNIVERSITY OF MASSACHUSETTS, AMHERST

THE CONFLICT BETWEEN CHURCH AND
STATE IN LATIN AMERICA*
Edited by Frederick B. Pike

THE MASTERS AND THE SLAVES (ABRIDGED) *
A STUDY IN THE DEVELOPMENT OF BRAZILIAN CIVILIZATION
By Gilberto Freyre

DO THE AMERICAS HAVE A COMMON HISTORY? *
A CRITIQUE OF THE BOLTON THEORY
Edited by Lewis Hanke

AMAZON TOWN
A STUDY OF MAN IN THE TROPICS
(With a New Epilogue by the Author)
By Charles Wagley

A VOYAGE TO SOUTH AMERICA (ABRIDGED) *
By Jorge Juan and Antonio de Ulloa
(With an Introduction by Irving A. Leonard)

AGRARIAN REFORM IN LATIN AMERICA
Edited by T. Lynn Smith

THE BANDEIRANTES
THE HISTORICAL ROLE OF THE BRAZILIAN PATHFINDERS
Edited by Richard M. Morse

DICTATORSHIP IN SPANISH AMERICA*
Edited by Hugh M. Hamill, Jr.

THE ORIGINS OF THE LATIN AMERICAN
REVOLUTIONS, 1808–1826 *
Edited by R. A. Humphreys and John Lynch

THE EXPULSION OF THE JESUITS FROM
LATIN AMERICA
Edited by Magnus Mörner

A Note on the Type

The text of this book was set on the Linotype in a type face called Baskerville. The face is a facsimile reproduction of types cast from molds made for John Baskerville (1706–75) from his designs. The punches for the revived Linotype Baskerville were cut under the supervision of the English printer George W. Jones. John Baskerville's original face was one of the forerunners of the type style known as "modern face" to printers—a "modern" of the period A.D. 1800.

Composed, printed, and bound by
The Colonial Press Inc., Clinton, Mass.